T0247037

PLAY ON SHAKESPEARE

All's Well That Ends Well

PLAY ON SHAKESPEARE

All's Well That Ends Well	Virginia Grise
Antony and Cleopatra	Christopher Chen
As You Like It	David Ivers
The Comedy of Errors	Christina Anderson
Coriolanus	Sean San José
Cymbeline	Andrea Thome
Edward III	Octavio Solis
Hamlet	Lisa Peterson
Henry IV	Yvette Nolan
Henry V	Lloyd Suh
Henry VI	Douglas P. Langworthy
Henry VIII	Caridad Svich
Julius Caesar	Shishir Kurup
King John	Brighde Mullins
King Lear	Marcus Gardley
Love's Labour's Lost	Josh Wilder
Macbeth	Migdalia Cruz
Measure for Measure	Aditi Brennan Kapil
The Merchant of Venice	Elise Thoron
The Merry Wives of Windsor	Dipika Guha
A Midsummer Night's Dream	Jeffrey Whitty
Much Ado About Nothing	Ranjit Bolt
Othello	Mfoniso Udofia
Pericles	Ellen McLaughlin
Richard II	Naomi Iizuka
Richard III	Migdalia Cruz
Romeo and Juliet	Hansol Jung
The Taming of the Shrew	Amy Freed
The Tempest	Kenneth Cavander
Timon of Athens	Kenneth Cavander
Titus Andronicus	Amy Freed
Troilus and Cressida	Lillian Groag
Twelfth Night	Alison Carey
The Two Gentlemen of Verona	Amelia Roper
The Two Noble Kinsmen	Tim Slover
The Winter's Tale	Tracy Young

All's Well That Ends Well

by
William Shakespeare

Modern verse translation by
Virginia Grise

Dramaturgy by
Natsuko Ohama

Arizona State University
Tempe, Arizona
2024

———

Publication of Play On Shakespeare is assisted by
generous support from the Hitz Foundation.
For more information, please visit www.playonshakespeare.org

———

Published by ACMRS Press
Arizona Center for Medieval and Renaissance Studies,
Arizona State University, Tempe, Arizona
www.acmrspress.com

Library of Congress Cataloging-in-Publication Data
Names: Grise, Virginia, author. | Ohama, Natsuko, contributor. |
  Shakespeare, William, 1564-1616. All's well that ends well
Title: All's well that ends well / by William Shakespeare ; modern verse
  translation by Virginia Grise ; dramaturgy by Natsuko Ohama.
Description: Tempe, Arizona : ACMRS Press, 2024. | Series: Play on
  Shakespeare | Summary: "One of Shakespeare's lesser-known plays
  translated into language for modern ears"-- Provided by publisher.
Identifiers: LCCN 2024031502 (print) | LCCN 2024031503 (ebook) |
  ISBN 9780866987875 (paperback) | ISBN 9780866987882 (ebook)
Subjects: LCSH: Runaway husbands--Drama. | Married women--Drama.
  | Florence (Italy)--Drama. | LCGFT: Comedy plays.
Classification: LCC PR2878.A45 G75 2024 (print) | LCC PR2878.A45
  (ebook) | DDC 812/.6--dc23/eng/20240708
LC record available at https://lccn.loc.gov/2024031502
LC ebook record available at https://lccn.loc.gov/2024031503

Printed in the United States of America

We wish to acknowledge our gratitude
for the extraordinary generosity of the
Hitz Foundation

∽

Special thanks to the Play On Shakespeare staff
Lue Douthit, President and Co-Founder
Taylor Bailey, Producing Director
Cheryl Rizzo, Business Director
Artie Calvert, Finance Director

∽

Originally commissioned by the
Oregon Shakespeare Festival
Bill Rauch, Artistic Director
Cynthia Rider, Executive Director

PLAY ON SHAKESPEARE

In 2015, the Oregon Shakespeare Festival announced a new commissioning program. It was called "Play on!: 36 playwrights translate Shakespeare." It elicited a flurry of reactions. For some people this went too far: "You can't touch the language!" For others, it didn't go far enough: "Why not new adaptations?" I figured we would be on the right path if we hit the sweet spot in the middle.

Some of the reaction was due not only to the scale of the project, but its suddenness: 36 playwrights, along with 38 dramaturgs, had been commissioned and assigned to translate 39 plays, and they were already hard at work on the assignment. It also came fully funded by the Hitz Foundation with the shocking sticker price of $3.7 million.

I think most of the negative reaction, however, had to do with the use of the word "translate." It's been difficult to define precisely. It turns out that there is no word for the kind of subtle and rigorous examination of language that we are asking for. We don't mean "word for word," which is what most people think of when they hear the word translate. We don't mean "paraphrase," either.

The project didn't begin with 39 commissions. Linguist John McWhorter's musings about translating Shakespeare is what sparked this project. First published in his 1998 book *Word on the Street* and reprinted in 2010 in *American Theatre* magazine, he notes that the "irony today is that the Russians, the French, and other people in foreign countries possess Shakespeare to a much greater extent than we do, for the simple reason that they get to enjoy Shakespeare in the language they speak."

This intrigued Dave Hitz, a long-time patron of the Oregon Shakespeare Festival, and he offered to support a project that looked at Shakespeare's plays through the lens of the English we speak today. How much has the English language changed since Shakespeare? Is it possible that there are conventions in the early modern English of Shakespeare that don't translate to us today, especially in the moment of hearing it spoken out loud as one does in the theater?

How might we "carry forward" the successful communication between actor and audience that took place 400 years ago? "Carry forward," by the way, is what we mean by "translate." It is the fourth definition of *translate* in the Oxford English Dictionary.

As director of literary development and dramaturgy at the Oregon Shakespeare Festival, I was given the daunting task of figuring out how to administer the project. I began with Kenneth Cavander, who translates ancient Greek tragedies into English. I figured that someone who does that kind of work would lend an air of seriousness to the project. I asked him how might he go about translating from the source language of early modern English into the target language of contemporary modern English?

He looked at different kinds of speech: rhetorical and poetical, soliloquies and crowd scenes, and the puns in comedies. What emerged from his tinkering became a template for the translation commission. These weren't rules exactly, but instructions that every writer was given.

First, do no harm. There is plenty of the language that doesn't need translating. And there is some that does. Every playwright had different criteria for assessing what to change.

Second, go line-by-line. No editing, no cutting, no "fixing." I want the whole play translated. We often cut the gnarly bits in

Shakespeare for performance. What might we make of those bits if we understood them in the moment of hearing them? Might we be less compelled to cut?

Third, all other variables stay the same: the time period, the story, the characters, their motivations, and their thoughts. We designed the experiment to examine the language.

Fourth, and most important, the language must follow the same kind of rigor and pressure as the original, which means honoring the meter, rhyme, rhetoric, image, metaphor, character, action, and theme. Shakespeare's astonishingly compressed language must be respected. Trickiest of all: making sure to work within the structure of the iambic pentameter.

We also didn't know which of Shakespeare's plays might benefit from this kind of investigation: the early comedies, the late tragedies, the highly poetic plays. So we asked three translators who translate plays from other languages into English to examine a Shakespeare play from each genre outlined in the *First Folio*: Kenneth took on *Timon of Athens,* a tragedy; Douglas Langworthy worked on the *Henry the Sixth* history plays, and Ranjit Bolt tried his hand at the comedy *Much Ado about Nothing.*

Kenneth's *Timon* received a production at the Alabama Shakespeare in 2014 and it was on the plane ride home that I thought about expanding the project to include 39 plays. And I wanted to do them all at once. The idea was to capture a snapshot of contemporary modern English. I couldn't oversee that many commissions, and when Ken Hitz (Dave's brother and president of the Hitz Foundation) suggested that we add a dramaturg to each play, the plan suddenly unfolded in front of me. The next day, I made a simple, but extensive, proposal to Dave on how to commission and develop 39 translations in three years. He responded immediately with "Yes."

My initial thought was to only commission translators who translate plays. But I realized that "carry forward" has other meanings. There was a playwright in the middle of the conversation 400 years ago. What would it mean to carry *that* forward?

For one thing, it would mean that we wanted to examine the texts through the lens of performance. I am interested in learning how a dramatist makes sense of the play. Basically, we asked the writers to create performable companion pieces.

I wanted to tease out what we mean by contemporary modern English, and so we created a matrix of writers who embodied many different lived experiences: age, ethnicity, gender-identity, experience with translations, geography, English as a second language, knowledge of Shakespeare, etc.

What the playwrights had in common was a deep love of language and a curiosity about the assignment. Not everyone was on board with the idea and I was eager to see how the experiment would be for them. They also pledged to finish the commission within three years.

To celebrate the completion of the translations, we produced a festival in June 2019 in partnership with The Classic Stage Company in New York to hear all 39 of them. Four hundred years ago I think we went to *hear* a play; today we often go to *see* a play. In the staged reading format of the Festival, we heard these plays as if for the first time. The blend of Shakespeare with another writer was seamless and jarring at the same time. Countless actors and audience members told us that the plays were understandable in ways they had never been before.

Now it's time to share the work. We were thrilled when Ayanna Thompson and her colleagues at the Arizona Center for Medieval and Renaissance Studies offered to publish the translations for us.

I ask that you think of these as marking a moment in time.

The editions published in this series are based on the scripts that were used in the Play on! Festival in 2019. For the purpose of the readings, there were cuts allowed and these scripts represent those reading drafts.

The original commission tasked the playwrights and dramaturg to translate the whole play. The requirement of the commission was for two drafts which is enough to put the ball in play. The real fun with these texts is when there are actors, a director, a dramaturg, and the playwright wrestling with them together in a rehearsal room.

The success of a project of this scale depends on the collaboration and contributions of many people. The playwrights and dramaturgs took the assignment seriously and earnestly and were humble and gracious throughout the development of the translations. Sally Cade Holmes and Holmes Productions, our producer since the beginning, provided a steady and calm influence.

We have worked with more than 1,200 artists in the development of these works. We have partnered with more than three dozen theaters and schools. Numerous readings and more than a dozen productions of these translations have been heard and seen in the United States as well as Canada, England, and the Czech Republic.

There is a saying in the theater that 80% of the director's job is taken care of when the production is cast well. Such was my luck when I hired Taylor Bailey, who has overseen every reading and workshop, and was the producer of the Festival in New York. Katie Kennedy has gathered all the essays, and we have been supported by the rest of the Play on Shakespeare team: Kamilah Long, Summer Martin, and Amrita Ramanan.

All of this has come to be because Bill Rauch, then artistic director of the Oregon Shakespeare Festival, said yes when Dave

Hitz pitched the idea to him in 2011. Actually he said, "Hmm, interesting," which I translated to "yes." I am dearly indebted to that 'yes.'

My gratitude to Dave, Ken, and the Hitz Foundation can never be fully expressed. Their generosity, patience, and unwavering belief in what we are doing has given us the confidence to follow the advice of Samuel Beckett: "Ever tried. Ever failed. No matter. Try again. Fail again. Fail better."

Play on!

Dr. Lue Douthit
CEO/Creative Director at Play on Shakespeare
October 2020

WHAT WAS I THINKING?
Natusko Ohama

A world away and time ago October 2017 I received an email from Lue Douthit inviting me to direct a workshop of *All's Well That Ends Well,* which she said was part of the Play on! Project she was overseeing. Translating Shakespeare.

What … had we fallen so far, the theatre plunging like a fallen angel into the ocean of language, drowning with atrophied wings unable to muster the strength to use an OED or rend meaning respectfully from the BARD? I like my Shakespeare straight up, no chasers. No nonsense in the nonsense. The First Folio or bust. Who did these PLAY ON People think they were playing?

For me the years of gauntlets thrown down, the Oxfordians, Stratfordians, bending obscure puns and pancakes, academics and actors, improvisation and pauses … tipped me into the OK what the hell. Is this a legitimate experiment?

(… As to the legitimate, fine word-legitimate

Well my legitimate, if this letter speed

And my invention thrive ….)

After all it was a curiosity, and I thought it would be good to spend time with *All's Well.* It was only a three-day workshop. It was playwright Virginia Grise and dramaturg Richard Bracho who were the team, along with 10 actresses. All actresses. Being quite at home from working decades with Lisa Wolpe and the LA Women's Shakespeare, I found this particular play suited to be interpreted by all women.

Bertram being much more palatable being held in the female understanding. The Countess giving modern insight into the mother hood, and modern (we think) support and morality of friendship and sympathy. Vicky working text side by side by text by side. Kept the major speeches intact, clarifying some phases and meaning. The playwright searching through the forests of her experience and life in all the concentric circles that make Shakespeare such a profound experience.

One starts with not knowing. Not understanding. Looking at versions.

Then wresting the meanings, looking in various stalls where the words are defined.

One munches on hay and oats.

Histories.

One thinks and sounds it out. Searching, personalizing, questioning, puzzling, pulling from the present parallel meanings, amusing ones self. Picking through the sense and senses. Great actors are always such an aid with this. Unafraid to ask what this means, stubborn to eke out the meaning, asking the questions. Massaging the phase with experience and exploration.

Vicky would go away. Munch on hay and oats.

Then come back, shy and fiery. New pages. I don't have my side by side notes anymore, and the PDF of versions no longer work. I do remember the feeling when a particular new modern phrase we were familiar with was added, clarifying an old archaic phrase, would appear. It gave that duality of joy and humor adding dimension that was not necessarily better, but fun. More direct. Less snobby. Clearer to us. Amusing. Those were the best moments.

Spilling the T.

The years went on. Life. Life happened. Projects intervened. I became her dramaturg. I am no legitimate dramaturg, I am an actor director coach, so possibly a match made in heaven. I know great dramaturgs and I have neither the intellect or the work ethic for it. With all the integrity of an unemployed actor, I accepted the assignment.

Lue held our hooves to the fire. We worked. We ate more hay and oats. Illnesses. Moves. Shakespeare is invincible. We would meet sporadically. Vicky and I met at USC. Also OSF? Correct me if I am wrong. Years flew.

Culminating at CSC in NY having come around the turn into the final stretch. It was the battle of Agincourt. All the tents and soldiers, camp to camp, the whole logical thing was fabulous.

Wonderful actresses. Subtle artful changes in text. The story was told. Artfully and beautifully I thought. You can see the versions if you ask Lue, I am sure. But who would? Perhaps a dried up academic who is picking through the rubble of the WHY and WHEREFORE, The fardel there? What's i' the fardel? Wherefore that box?

The plays are meant to be played. If it brings kids in closer, bring it on.

Music being the food of love. Words the nourishment. And the playing, the satisfaction of love, PLAY ON!

CHARACTERS IN THE PLAY

(in order of speaking)

COUNTESS OF ROUSSILLON, Bertram's mother

BERTRAM, the Count of Roussillon

LAFEU, an old lord

HELEN, a gentlewoman protected by the Countess

PAROLES, Bertram's follower

KING OF FRANCE

1 DUMAINE

2 DUMAINE

REYNALDO, the Countess's steward

LAVATCH, a clown in the Countess's household

DUKE OF FLORENCE

WIDOW CAPILET, an old widow in Florence

DIANA, the Widow's daughter

MARIANA, the Widow's neighbor and friend

INTERPRETER

FRENCH GENTLEMAN

EPILOGUE

Other Lords, Attendants, a Page, Soldiers, Trumpeters, a Drummer, Citizens, and Guards

ACT 1 ♦ SCENE 1

ROUSSILLON. THE COUNT'S PALACE.

Bertram (Count of Roussillon), the Countess (his mother), Helen,
and Lord Lafeu enter, dressed in black. They are in mourning.

COUNTESS

In delivering my son from me I bury a second husband.

BERTRAM

And in going, mother, I weep o'er my father's death anew; but
I must attend to his majesty's command, now his ward, he
rules over me.

LAFEU

You shall find of the King a husband, madam; you, sir, a   5
father. A man so good to everyone must, without question,
be good to you whose worthiness would stir it up where it
wanted, rather than lack it where there is such abundance.

COUNTESS

What hope is there of his majesty's condition?

LAFEU

He has abandoned his physicians, madam. Thinking he   10
could buy time under their watch; instead, over time, he's
only lost hope.

COUNTESS

This young gentlewoman had a father — *had*: How sad a
word, how sad a passage from *has* to *had*, from life to death.
He as skilled as he was honest, so gifted, had it stretched so   15
far, would have made nature immortal, and death should
have play for lack of work. For the King's sake, if he were living, I think it would be the death of the King's disease.

1

LAFEU

What was his name, the man you speak of, madam?

COUNTESS

Gerard from Narbonne. He was famous, sir, in his profes- 20
sion, and rightfully so.

LAFEU

Excellent indeed, madam. The King most recently spoke of
him, admiringly — and mournfully. If his knowing could go
toe to toe against mortality, he was skillful enough to have
lived, now as before, perhaps always, but knowledge is no 25
match for death.

BERTRAM

What is it, my good lord, the King languishes of?

LAFEU

A fistula, my lord.

BERTRAM

A what?

LAFEU

A swelling of the heart, my lord. 30

BERTRAM

I have never heard of that before.

LAFEU

I wish no one had. Was this gentlewoman the daughter of
Gerard from Narbonne?

COUNTESS

His only child, my lord, and bequeathed to my overlooking. I
have high hopes for her future that good education promises; 35
she inherits her personality and good character which makes
fair gifts fairer. For where an unclean mind carries virtuous
qualities, there commendations go with pity; they are virtues
but they don't go unsullied. In her, they are the better because
of her innocence. She inherits her honesty and achieves her 40

goodness.

LAFEU

Your compliments, madam, get tears from her. She is crying now.

COUNTESS

It's the best brine a young woman can season her praise in. The remembrance of her father never approaches her heart 45 but the tyranny of her sorrows takes all livelihood from her cheek. That's enough, Helen. C'mon, that's enough. You don't want people to think you're putting on a show, do you?

HELEN

A show perhaps but these tears, these tears are real.

LAFEU

Moderate lamentation is the right of the dead; excessive grief, 50 the enemy to the living.

COUNTESS

If the living be not enemy to the grief, the excess makes it soon mortal.

BERTRAM (*impatiently interrupting*)

Madam, I would like your blessing.

LAFEU

What do you mean? 55

COUNTESS

You are blessed, Bertram, and succeed your father
In manners as in shape! Your blood and virtue
Contend for empire in you, and your goodness
Is yours to command.

(*she takes a ring off her hand and gifts it to her son*)

Love all, trust few, 60
Do wrong to none. And be prepared for war
But not the first to draw, defend your friends
With your own life. Be careful what you say

3

But speak up when you must. What heaven more will,
That you may supply and my prayers pluck down   65
Fall on your head. Farewell, my son.
(*to Lafeu*) He's an unseasoned courtier; good my lord,
Advise him well.

LAFEU

He cannot want the best
That shall attend his love.   70

COUNTESS

Heaven bless him! — Farewell, Bertram.

BERTRAM (*rising*)

The best wishes that can be forged in your thoughts be servants
to you.

The Countess exits

BERTRAM (*to Helen*)

Be consoling to my mother, your mistress; take good care of
her.

LAFEU

What you must take good care of, Helen, is your father's reputation. Farewell, pretty lady.   75

Bertram and Lafeu exit, leaving Helen, alone, or so she thinks.
Reynaldo listens from a distance, unseen.

HELEN

O, were that all! I think not on my father,
And these great tears grace his remembrance more
Than those I shed for him at his death.
What was he like?
I have forgot him. My imagination   80
Carries no favor in 't but Bertram's.
I am undone. There is no living, none,
If Bertram be away. 'Twere all one
That I should love a bright particular star,

4

And think to wed it, he — so high above me.   85
He. The sun, the moon. He. The Earth.
He. The center of the universe — remains still.
And I orbit round and round. Circle. Circle. He.
In his bright radiance and collateral light,
Must I be comforted, not in his sphere.   90
The ambition in my love thus plagues itself.
The doe that would be mated by the lion
Must die for love. It's pretty but a plague,
To see him every hour, to sit and draw
His arch-ed eye brows, his piercing eyes, his curls,   95
On the canvas of my heart etched — too capable
Of every line and trick of his sweet favor.
But now he's gone, and my idolatrous fancy
Must sanctify his relics and other traces of his presence.
Who comes here?   100

       Paroles enters. Reynaldo exits catlike, unseen.

(*aside*) One of his men.
I love him for Bertram's sake —
And yet I know him to be a notorious liar,
Think him a great fool, an absolute coward.
Yet bad — bad never looked so good.   105
Which finds shelter while virtue's steely bones
Look bleak i' the cold wind.
Cold wisdom waiting on superfluous folly.

PAROLES

Good day, fair queen.

HELEN

Good day to you, monarch.   110

PAROLES

No.

HELEN

And no.

PAROLES

Are you meditating on virginity?

HELEN

Indeed I am. You are something of a soldier, let me ask you a question. Man is the enemy to virginity: How may we *barri-* 115 *cad-o* it against him?

PAROLES

Keep him out. You must fortify yourself.

HELEN

But he strikes, and our virginity, though valiant in the defense, is still weak. Tell me, soldier, how to resist his advances.

PAROLES

There is no way. Man will lay siege to surround you, under- 120 mine you, take it from you, fill you up, and — if you are not careful — make your belly blow up.

HELEN

May God keep our poor virginity safe from the underminers and men that blow. Is there is no military strategy that allows for virgins to undermine *them*, to knock *them* up — to blow 125 up men?

PAROLES

Try to blow down virginity and see how quickly he blows up. Blow him — down again — you lose the war by opening the breach. His soldiers will launch a frontal assault — blow up your city. It is not politic in the commonwealth of nature to 130 preserve virginity. There was never a virgin born to a virgin. Virgins are not born unless virginity is lost. You were per- fectly made — to make virgins. Virginity by being once lost may be ten times found; try to hold it tight, it is lost forever. Too cold a companion, away with it already. 135

HELEN

I will defend it a little longer, even if I have to die a virgin.

PAROLES

There's little that can be said in its defense. 'Tis against the very law of nature. To speak in defense of virginity, is to accuse your own mothers — not one of them a virgin and to attack your mother is the worse type of disobedience. No 140 different than suicide: Virginity kills itself, and should be buried on the side of the road, in an unmarked grave, as a desperate offendress against nature. Virginity, much like a cheese, breeds mites; consumes itself to the very paring, and so dies, feeding on its own stubborn pride. Besides, virginity 145 is testy, proud, idle, made of self-love — the most prohibited sin in the canon. Don't hold onto it. You have no other choice but to lose it. Let it go! Within a year it will make itself two, which is a goodly increase, and the principal itself not much worse. Away with it I say. 150

HELEN

What might one do, sir, to lose it to her own liking?

PAROLES

Let me see. You could marry someone of your own choosing on your own accord. But remember: Virginity is a commodity, girl. It will — in time — lose its shine: The longer you keep it, the less it is worth. Off with it while you can still get 155 a good return. Virginity, old fashioned, is just so last season, richly suited but unsuitable. Give it up when you are asked. Your date, sweet, is better in your pie and your porridge than in your cheek, and your virginity — your old, tired virginity — is like one of our French withered pears — it looks sick; it 160 tastes dry. It is a withered pear after all. It was better before, of course — but now it is just a withered pear. Now tell me — what are you going to do with it?

HELEN

    In my virgin love, which is not yet a withered pear —

    There your master shall have a thousand loves,   165

    A mother and a mistress and a friend,

    A phoenix, a captain, and an enemy,

    A guide, a goddess, and a sovereign,

    A counselor, a traitress, someone dear:

    His humble ambition, proud humility,   170

    His jarring concord and his soothing discord

    His faith, his sweet disaster, with a world

    Of pretty fond adopted namings

    That blinking Cupid gossips. Now shall he —

    I know not what he will have. God bless him.   175

    The court is a place where one learns and he is one —

PAROLES

    — Ay Dios mio. Who are you talking about?

HELEN

    I wish him well. It is a shame.

PAROLES

    What's a shame?

HELEN

    That wishing well is nothing but a wish.   180

    There's not a body in it

    Which might be felt. That we — the poorer born —

    Whose baser stars confine us to only wishes.

    Think but act not on our desire,

    Which never returns us thanks.   185

A Page enters

PAGE

    Monsieur Paroles, Lord Bertram calls for you.

Page exits

8

PAROLES

Little Helen, farewell. If I can remember you, I will think of
you at court.

HELEN

Monsieur Paroles, you were born under a lucky star.

PAROLES

Under Mars, actually.   190

HELEN

Of course.

PAROLES

Why of course?

HELEN

Mars, the Roman God of War. You are a soldier, are you not?
It's only logical you would be born under the red star.

PAROLES

When he was predominant.   195

HELEN

When he was in retrograde rather. Or so I think.

PAROLES

Why do you think so?

HELEN

Because you back-peddle when you fight.

PAROLES

That's for advantage.

HELEN

So is running away, when fear proposes the safety. But the   200
composition that your valor and fear make in you is a virtue
of a good wing, and I like the wear well.

PAROLES

I have much business to attend to, far too busy to answer you.
I will come back a perfect courtier, and I will thrust upon
you all the ways of the court so that you will be prepared   205

for a courtier's counsel and understand the advice I have to give you; or you will die alone and ungrateful, and isolated by your ignorance. Farewell. When you are free, say your prayers; when you are not, remember your friends. Find you a good husband and use him as he uses you. Again farewell. 210
Farewell again.

Paroles exits

HELEN

We are masters of our own fate.
Our remedies oft in ourselves do lie
Which we ascribe to heaven. The fated sky
Gives us free scope, only does backward pull   215
Our slow designs when we ourselves are dull.
What power is it which mounts my love so high,
That makes me see and cannot feed mine eye?
The mightiest space in fortune nature brings
To join like likes and kiss like native things.   220
Impossible be strange attempts to those
That weigh their pains in sense and do suppose
What has been cannot be. Whoever strove
To show her merit that did miss her love?
The King's disease — my project may deceive me,   225
But my intentions are fixed and will not leave me.

Helen exits

ACT 1 ◆ SCENE 2
PARIS. THE KING'S PALACE.

A flourish of cornets

King enters with letters, with 1 Dumaine and 2 Dumaine

KING

The Florentines and Sienese still at each others' throats.
They've both put up a fight and war wages on.

10

1 DUMAINE

So it's reported, sir.

KING

No, it's most credible. We here receive

A certainty vouched from our cousin Austria,   5

With caution that the Florentine will ask us

For speedy aid — wherein our dearest friend

Prejudices the business, and would seem

To have us make denial.

1 DUMAINE

You trust his love and wisdom.   10

We should listen.

KING

He has armed our answer

And Florence is denied before they ask

Yet for our gentlemen that mean to see

The Tuscan service, freely they have leave   15

To fight for either side.

2 DUMAINE

It may serve as

Good schooling for our young men, who all thirst

For fresh air and adventure.

KING

Who's he comes here?   20

Bertram, Lafeu, and Paroles enter

1 DUMAINE

It is the Count Roussillon, my good lord,

Young Bertram.

KING (*to Bertram*)

Youth, you bear your father's face.

Frank nature, rather curious than in haste,

Has well composed you. May you inherit   25

Your father's moral parts. Welcome to Paris.

BERTRAM

My thanks and duty are your majesty's.

KING

I wish I was as fit and healthy now,
As when your father and myself in friendship
First tried our soldiership. He did look far   30
Into the service of the time, and was
Discipled of the bravest. He lasted long,
But on us both did haggish age steal on,
And wore us out of act. It much repairs me
To talk of your good father; in his youth   35
He had a wit which I can well observe
Today in our young lords; except their jokes
Are often returned at their own expense.
Ere they can hide their levity in honor.
He was courteous, exhibited pride   40
Without contempt, and sharpness without bitterness.
His equal had awaked them, and his honor,
Clock to itself, knew the true minute when
Exception bid him speak, and at this time
His tongue obeyed his hand. Who were below him   45
He viewed as creatures of a better place,
And bow'd his eminent top to their low ranks.
Making them proud of his humility,
In their poor praise he humbled. Such a man
Might show today's men a thing or two,   50
Which, followed well, would demonstrate them now
Just how far behind they have fallen.

BERTRAM

His good remembrance, sir,
Lies richer in your thoughts than on his tomb;

No finer words writ in his epitaph   55
Than in your royal speech.
KING
    If I were with him! He would always say —
    Me thinks I hear him now; his plausive words
    He scattered not in ears, but grafted them
    To grow there and to bear. "Let me not live" —   60
    This his good melancholy oft began
    On the catastrophe and heel of pastime;
    When it was out — "Let me not live," he'd say,
    "After my flame lacks oil, to be the snuff
    Of younger spirits, whose apprehensive senses   65
    All but new things disdain, whose judgements are
    Mere fathers of their garments, whose constancies
    Expire before their fashions." This he wish'd.
    I wish it too.
    Since I no wax nor honey can bring home   70
    I quickly will be extracted from my hive.
    To give some laborers' room.
2 DUMAINE
    You're loved, sir.
    Those that show it least will miss you most.
KING
    I'm taking up space, I know't. How long is't, count,   75
    Since your father's physician died?
    He was well known.
BERTRAM
    It's been six months, my lord.
KING
    If he were still alive I would go see him.
    Lend me a hand.   80
    The other doctors have worn me out with all their medications.

Nature and sickness are fighting it out on their own time.

Welcome, count. You are like a son to me.

BERTRAM

Thank you, your majesty.

All exit. Flourish.

ACT 1 ♦ SCENE 3

BACK IN ROUSSILLON. THE COUNT'S PALACE.

The Countess enters with her steward Reynaldo
Lavatch follows behind

COUNTESS

I will listen to you now. What do you say about young Helen?

REYNALDO

Madam, I hope that my actions speak louder than words and
show all that I have done to make you happy. To speak of these
good deeds myself would hurt my modesty and make me less
deserving of your praise.   5

COUNTESS

What is this buffoon doing here? (*to Lavatch*) Get you gone,
clown. I don't believe all the terrible things people say about
you but I know you lack not foolishness to commit the things
they say. I should know better — folly and mischief are your
mistress.   10

LAVATCH

Well then — you see me, madam. I am a poor fellow.

COUNTESS

Well, sir?

LAVATCH

No, madam, 'tis not so well that I am poor, though many of
the rich be damned; but if I may have your ladyship's good
will to marry, go out to the world — to do as I may — Isbel   15
— the woman and I — will do as we can.

COUNTESS

Will you need to become a beggar?

LAVATCH

I do beg your good will in this case.

COUNTESS

In what case?

LAVATCH

In my and Isbel's case. I own nothing, and I think I shall never   20
have the blessing of God 'till I have children of my own. They
say babies are blessings.

COUNTESS

Tell me the reason you want to marry.

LAVATCH

My poor body, madam, requires it. I am driven by the flesh
and lust. The devil's in the driver's seat.   25

COUNTESS

Is this your only reason?

LAVATCH

Trust, madam, I have other holy reasons, such as they are.

COUNTESS

May the world know them?

LAVATCH

I have been wicked, madam — a wicked, wicked creature,
and indeed — I do marry so that I might repent.   30

COUNTESS

You will regret your marriage much sooner than you will
repent your wickedness.

LAVATCH

I ain't got no friends, madam. I hope to gain one or two from
my wife.

COUNTESS

Friends like that are your enemies, fool.   35

LAVATCH

Uh — madam. You are shallow. You don't know what great
friends I have. Me and my … They come and do the things
I am sick and tired of doing. Me and my … He that ploughs
my land, spares me labor, but lets me reap the benefits of his
crop. Me and my … If I am his cuckold, he is my drudge. Me   40
and my friends. He that comforts my wife is the cherisher
of my flesh and blood. He that cherishes my flesh and blood
loves my flesh and blood. He that loves my flesh and blood
is my friend. Man and wife is one flesh. Ergo, he that kisses
my wife, Me and my friends. He that pleasures my wife, Me   45
and my friends. He that beds my wife Is. My. Friend. If men
could be satisfied to just be what they are — cuckolds — they
would not fear marriage.

COUNTESS

Will you forever be a foul-mouthed and malicious scoundrel?

LAVATCH

I am a prophet, madam, and I spit truth in my own way.   50
For I the ballad will repeat
Which men full true shall find:
Your marriage comes by destiny,
Your cuckoo sings by kind.

COUNTESS

Get, get, get you gone. I will talk with you more later.   55

REYNALDO

If it's ok with you, madam, might he summon Helen here to
you? I'm going to tell you about her.

COUNTESS (*to Lavatch*)

Tell my gentlewoman I want to speak with her. Helen, I mean.

LAVATCH

Was this fair face the cause, quoth she,
Why the Grecians sacked Troy?   60

Fond done, done fond,
Was this King Priam's joy?
With that she sighed as she stood,
With that she sighed as she stood,
And gave this sentence then: 65
Among nine bad if one be good,
Among nine bad if one be good,
There's yet one good in ten.

COUNTESS

What, "one good in ten"? You corrupt the song, clown.

LAVATCH

One good woman in ten, madam, which makes the song   70
better. If God would be so fair! We'd find no fault with the
tithe-woman if I were the parson. One in ten, I say! If a good
woman was born every time there was a shooting star or at
an earthquake, we'd all be lucky. A man could rip his heart
out before he gets him a good woman.   75

COUNTESS

Get out of here, you miscreant, and do what I told you to do.

LAVATCH

That man should be at woman's command, and yet no harm
done! Though honesty is not always proper, yet it will do no
harm; it will wear the white tunic of humility over the black
gown of a big heart. Well then, I am going now. The business 80
is for Helen to come hither.

Lavatch exits

COUNTESS

Well, now.

REYNALDO

I know, madam, you love your gentlewoman completely.

COUNTESS

Indeed, I do. Her father bequeathed her to me, and because

she herself, without other advantage, has little else, deserves 85
as much love as she finds. There is more owing her than is
paid, and more shall be paid her than she'll demand.

REYNALDO

Madam, recently I was closer to her than I think she wish'd
me; she was alone, or so she thought. From her mouth to
God's ears, she said she loved your son. Fortune, she said, was 90
no goddess, that put such difference between their class and
status; and love no god, if he only extends his might where
qualities were level. This she deliver'd with the most bitter
touch of sorrow that I have ever heard a virgin exclaim; I
thought it my duty to tell you this as soon as I could, seeing 95
as this is a matter of concern to you.

COUNTESS

You have spilled the tea and have done so rightly but keep
it to yourself. Many likelihoods inform'd me of this before,
which hung so teetering in the balance that I could neither
believe nor misdoubt. Leave me now. Keep this close to your 100
chest, and I thank you for your honest care. I will speak with
you further later.

Reynaldo exits

Helen enters

COUNTESS (*aside*)

Even so it was with me when I was young.
If ever we are nature's, these are ours; this thorn
Does to our rose of youth rightly belong;   105
Our blood to us, this to our blood is born.
It is the show and seal of nature's truth,
Where love's strong passion is impressed in youth.
By our remembrances of days long gone,
Such were our faults — though then we thought them none. 110
She is sick with love. I can see it now.

HELEN

   What is your pleasure, madam?

COUNTESS

   You know, Helen.

   I am a mother to you.

HELEN

   My honorable mistress. 115

COUNTESS

   No, a mother.

   Why not a mother? When I said "a mother"

   It looked like you saw a snake. What's in "mother"

   That makes you back away? I say I am your mother,

   And put you in the catalogue of those 120

   That were emwombed mine. Tis often seen

   Adoption strives with nature and choice breeds

   A native slip to us from foreign seeds

   You never oppressed me with a mother's groan

   Yet I express to you a mother's care. 125

   God's mercy, maiden! Does it curd your blood

   To say I am your mother? What's the matter?

   Why do you cry?

   Because you are my daughter?

HELEN

   That I am not. 130

COUNTESS

   I say I am your mother.

HELEN

   Pardon, madam.

   The Count Roussillon cannot be my brother.

   I from humble means, he from honored name;

   My parents own nothing, he is from nobility. 135

   He is my master, my dear lord, and I

Live as his servant and will die the same.
He must not be my brother.

COUNTESS

Nor I your mother?

HELEN

I wish you were my mother, madam. 140
But my lord, your son, were not my brother—
Indeed my mother! Or if mother
To us both, I'd give up my place in heaven,
So I were not his sister. Can't no other—
If I'm your daughter, must he be my brother? 145

COUNTESS

Yes, Helen, you could be my daughter-in-law.
I hope you don't mean it! "Daughter" and "mother"
Make your blood boil. What, pale again?
My fear has catched your fondness. Now I see
The mystery of your loneliness and find 150
The source of your salty tears. It's obvious:
You love my son. Invention is asham'd
Against the proclamation of your passion
To say you do not. Therefore tell me true;
And tell me now it's true; for look, your cheeks 155
Confess, one to the other, and your eyes
See it so grossly shown in your behaviours.
That in their kind they speak it. Only sin
And hellish obstinacy tie your tongue,
For fear that I will know the truth. Speak, is this true? 160
If it is true, you've spun a tangled thread;
If it is not, deny it, but I charge you
As heaven shall work in me for your avail,
To tell me the truth.

HELEN

Good madam, I am sorry.   165

COUNTESS

Do you love my son?

HELEN

Forgive me, noble mistress.

COUNTESS

Do you love my son?

HELEN

Don't you love him, madam?

COUNTESS

Go not around it. My love is a bond   170

Whereof the world takes note. Come, come, disclose

The state of your affection. Say how you feel.

Your passion is obvious.

HELEN

Then I confess,

Here on my knees, before high heaven and you,   175

I love your son.

My friends were poor but honest; so is my love.

Be not offended, for it hurts him not

That he is loved by me. I do not chase him

By any token of presumptuous suit,   180

Nor would I have him till I deserve him,

Although I do not know when that will be.

I know I love in vain, strive against hope;

Yet still I pour the waters of my love

Into a quibbling and rejective sieve   185

And still there is more to pour. I adore

The sun that looks upon his worshipper

But does not know him. My dearest madam.

Let not your hate of me challenge my love

For loving one you love; but if yourself,   190
Whose aged honor cites a virtuous youth,
Did ever, in so true a flame of liking,
Wish chastely and love dearly, that your Diane
Was both herself and Love — Oh then give pity
To her whose state is such that cannot choose   195
But lend and give where she is sure to lose;
Who seeks not to find what her search implies,
But riddle-like lives sweetly where she dies.

COUNTESS
Had you not lately an intent — speak truly —
To go to Paris?   200

HELEN
Madam, I had.

COUNTESS
Why? Tell the truth.

HELEN
I'll tell the truth, by grace itself I swear.
You know my father left me medicine
Of rare and prov'd effects, such as his reading   205
And manifest experience had collected
For general sovereignty; and that he willed me
In heedfull'st reservation to bestow them,
As notes whose faculties inclusive were
More than they were in note. Amongst them,   210
There is a proven remedy, set down,
To cure the desperate languishings whereof
The King is rendered lost.

COUNTESS
This was your motive
For Paris, was it? Speak.   215

HELEN

    My lord your son made me think about this;

    Else Paris, the medicine, and the King

    Would never cross my mind.

COUNTESS

    But, Helen do you think

    If you should offer your suppose-ed aid,   220

    He would accept it? He and his physicians

    Are of one mind: he, that they cannot help;

    And they, that they cannot help. Why listen

    To a poor unlearn-ed girl when none of them

    Can figure out what is wrong and have let   225

    The illness run its course.

HELEN

    There's more to it,

    More than my father's skill, which was the greatest

    Of his profession. It is my legacy

    Blessed by the luckiest stars in heaven.   230

    And if you would allow me to try it,

    I bet this life of mine on his grace's cure

    To the day, and hour.

COUNTESS

    You really believe this?

HELEN

    Oh, madam, I know it.   235

COUNTESS

    Why, Helen, you have my blessing and love,

    With money and attendants, and access

    To those of mine in court. I'll stay at home

    And pray to God for what you will attempt.

    Be gone tomorrow, and be sure of this: 240

    That I will do anything to help you.

ACT 2 ◆ SCENE 1

PARIS. THE KING'S PALACE.

A flourish of trumpets. The King enters carried in a chair,
with the two Lords Dumaine, Bertram, and Paroles.

KING

Farewell, young lords. These warlike principles
Do not throw from you. And you, my lords, farewell.
Share the advice amongst you; if both gain all,
The gift will stretch itself as 'tis received,
And is enough for both.   5

1 DUMAINE

It's our hope, sir,
That after we return from soldiering
We find your grace in health.

KING

No, no, it cannot be — and yet my heart
Will not confess he owns the malady   10
That does besiege my life. Farewell, young lords.
Whether I live or die, be you the sons
Of worthy Frenchmen; let Higher Italy—
Those bated that inherit but the fall
Of the last monarchy — make sure you come   15
Not to flirt with honor but to wed it when
The bravest knight falls back. Find what you seek,
That fame may cry your name. I say farewell.

1 DUMAINE

Health at your bidding serve your majesty.

KING

Watch out for those Italian girls. Take heed;   20

They say our French lack language to deny
If they demand. Beware of being captives
Before you serve.

1 DUMAINE

We take your warnings to heart.

KING

Farewell. (*to some Lords*) Stay back with me.   25

> *The King retires, with some Lords*

1 DUMAINE (*to Bertram*)

O my sweet lord, why must you stay behind?

PAROLES

It's not his fault. He is just a boy.

1 DUMAINE

Oh these brave wars.

PAROLES

Most admirable! I have seen those wars.

BERTRAM

I am commanded here, frustrated with "Too young" and   30
"Next year" and "It's too soon."

PAROLES

And your mind stand to 't, boy, steal away bravely.

BERTRAM

I will stay here, a show horse for the women,
Cooling my heels on the plain masonry,
Till honor be bought up, and no sword worn   35
But one to dance with. By God, I'll steal away.

1 DUMAINE

There's honor in the theft.

PAROLES

Just do it, Count.

2 DUMAINE

I, your partner in crime. And so, farewell.

BERTRAM

All for one and one for all. Our parting is a tortured body. 40

1 DUMAINE

Farewell, captain.

2 DUMAINE

Sweet Monsieur Paroles.

PAROLES

Noble heroes, my sword and yours are kin. Good sparks and
lustrous — a word — good men. You will find in the regiment of the Spinii a Captain Spurio. I call him Non-Auten- 45
tico. He has a scar. A war wound, on his sinister left cheek.
It was this very sword that etched it. Say to him I live, and
observe his response for me.

1 DUMAINE

We will, noble captain.

PAROLES

The God of War calls on you to serve him. 50

Both Lords Dumaine exit

PAROLES (*to Bertram*)

What will you do?

BERTRAM

Sssssh. The King.

The King re-enters

PAROLES

Pay more attention to the noble lords. You have restrained
yourself with too cold an adieu. Be more expressive to them,
for they wear themselves in the cap of time, they are in step 55
and set the pace; eat, speak, and move under the influence
of the most received star — and though the devil leads the
dance, still you must follow. Go after them, and give them an
extended farewell.

BERTRAM

And so I will. 60

PAROLES

Worthy fellows; and will likely prove most strapping swords-
men.

Bertram and Paroles exit

Lafeu enters

LAFEU (*to the King, kneeling*)

Forgive me, my lord, for me and for the news I bring.

KING

I'll pay you to stand up.

LAFEU (*rising*)

Then here's a man that stands who's brought his pardon. 65

I would you had kneeled, my lord, to ask me mercy,

And that at my bidding you would so stand up.

KING

I would if I could, and if I could I would

Then break your head. And asked your mercy for 't.

LAFEU

Good faith, touché! 70

But my good lord, 'tis thus: Will you be cured

Of your infirmity?

KING

No.

LAFEU

Oh, will you eat

No grapes, my royal fox? But yes you'll eat 75

My noble grapes, and if my royal fox

Could reach them. I have seen medicine

That's able to breathe life into a stone,

And make you sing and shout and dance the fox trot

With sprightly fire and motion; whose simple touch 80

Is potent enough to raise King Pepin, no,
To give great Charlemagne a pen in hand,
And write to her a love-line.

KING

What "her" is this?

LAFEU

Why, Doctor She. My lord, there's one arrived,   85
If you will see her. Now by my faith and honor,
If I may speak my thoughts seriously
Within my light deliverance, I have spoke
With one, that in her sex, her years, profession,
Wisdom and trueness, has amazed me more   90
Than I dare blame my weakness. Will you see her —
For that is her demand — and know her business?
That done, laugh well at me.

KING

Now, good Lafeu,
Bring in this miracle doctor you hold   95
In high esteem so we can be in awe
Like you. Or challenge you by questioning
Why she is now the apple of your eye?

LAFEU

No, I'll show you.
And not take all day either.   100

He goes to the door

KING

He always makes a big deal out of nothing.

Helen enters, wearing a disguise

LAFEU (*to Helen*)

Now, come this way.

KING

This haste has wings indeed.

29

LAFEU

    Now, come your ways.

    This is his majesty; say your mind to him.   105

    You do look like a traitor, but such traitors

    His majesty seldom fears; I am Cressid's uncle

    That dares leave you together. Fare you well.

           All exit but the King and Helen

KING

    Now, fair one, does your business have anything to do with us?

HELEN

    Yes, my good lord,   110

    Gerard de Narbonne was my father;

    Well known for what he did profess.

KING

    I knew him.

HELEN

    Then rather will I spare my praising him;

    Knowing him is enough. On his death bed,   115

    He gave me many remedies, but one

    Became the dearest issue of his practice,

    And of his vast experience his only darling,

    He made me guard it, as if my third eye,

    More dear than my own two, which I have done.   120

    And hearing your high majesty is touched

    With that malignant cause wherein the honor

    Of my dear father's gift stands chief in power,

    I come to tender it — and care for you.

    With all humility.   125

KING

    We thank you, maiden,

    But I don't have much faith in this your cure,

    When our most learned doctors leave us, and

The college of physicians has concluded
Despite their efforts they cannot stop nature   130
From running its course. I say we must not
So stain our judgement or corrupt our hope,
To prostitute our past-cure malady
To quacks or phonies; to dissever so
Our great self and our credit, to esteem   135
A senseless help, when help past sense we deem.

HELEN

My duty then shall pay me for my pains.
I will no longer force my office on you,
Humbly entreating from your royal thoughts
A modest one to bear me back again.   140

KING

I cannot give you less. It would be ungrateful.
You thought to help me, and such thanks I give
As one near death to those that wish him live.
But what I know full well, you know no part;
I knowing all my peril, you no art.   145

HELEN

What I can do, can do no hurt to try,
Since you're convinced there is no remedy.
He that of greatest works is finisher
Oft does them by the weakest minister.
So holy writ in babes has judgement shown   150
When judges have been babes; great floods have flown
From simple sources, and great seas have dried.
When miracles have by the greatest been denied
Our expectations fail us, most often
Where most it promises, and often hits   155
Where hope is coldest and despair most fits.

KING

I must not hear you. Fare you well, kind maid.
Your pains, not used, must still themselves be paid:
Proffers not took reap thanks for their reward.

HELEN

Inspirèd merit so by breath is barred.   160
It is not so with Him that all things knows
As it's with us that square our guess by shows;
But most it is presumption in us when
We count divine help as the act of men.
Dear sir, to my endeavors give consent.   165
Of heaven, not me, make an experiment.
I am not an impostor, that proclaim
Myself against the level of my aim,
But know I think, and think I know most sure,
My art is not past power, nor you past cure.   170

KING

Are you that confident? Within what space
Hope you my cure?

HELEN

With all the greatest grace,
"Ere twice the horses of the sun shall bring
Their fiery coacher his diurnal ring,   175
Ere twice in murk and occidental damp
Moist Hesperus hath quench'd her sleepy lamp,
Or four and twenty times the pilot's glass
Hath told the thievish minutes how they pass,
What is infirm from your sound parts shall fly,   180
Health shall live free, and sickness freely die."

KING

Upon your certainty and confidence
What dare you wager?

HELEN

    A horrible penalty.

    A strumpet's boldness, a divulged shame;   185

    Sung in odious ballads, my maiden's name

    Seared otherwise, no — worse of worst — extended

    With vilest torture, let my life be ended.

KING

    I think in you some blessed spirit does speak.

    His powerful sound within an organ weak;   190

    And what impossibility would slay

    In common sense, sense saves another way.

    Your life is dear, for that life can rate

    Worth name of life in you has estimate:

    Youth, beauty, wisdom, courage — all   195

    That happiness and prime can happy call.

    That you will risk your life must intimate

    Skill infinite or monstrous desperate.

    Sweet practitioner, your potion I'll try,

    That sentences you to death if I die.   200

HELEN

    If I break time, or flinch, and make a lie

    Of what I spoke, unpitied let me die,

    And well deserv'd. Not helping, death's my fee;

    But if I help, what do you promise me?

KING

    Make your demand.   205

HELEN

    But will you make it even?

KING

    Yes, by my scepter and my hopes of heaven.

HELEN

    Then will you give me with your kingly hand

Whatever husband that I will command:
Exempted be from me the arrogance 210
To choose forth from the royal blood of France,
My low and humble name to propagate
With any branch or image of your state;
But such a one, your subject, whom I know
Is free for me to ask, you to bestow. 215

KING

You have my word. The premises observed,
Based on my rallying you will be serv'd.
So make the choice of when's the time, for I,
Your resolv'd patient, on you still rely.
I should question you more and more I must 220
Though more to know could not be more to trust:
Where did you come from, who raised you but rest
Assured you're welcome, and undoubted blessed.
Give me some help here, ho! If you proceed
I give you my word, I shall match your deed 225

Flourish. The King, carried, exits with Helen.

ACT 2 ♦ SCENE 2
ROUSSILLON. THE COUNT'S PALACE.

The Countess and Lavatch enter

COUNTESS

Come on, sir-clown. I am now going to put your social skills
and upbringing to the test.

LAVATCH

I will prove myself highly fed but lowly taught. I know my
business is to serve the court.

COUNTESS

"To serve the court?" What makes you so special, that you 5
put that off with such contempt — "To serve the court"!

LAVATCH

Truly, madam, if God gives us just an ounce of manners —
any fool can get by at court with small gestures, just as long
as he don't speak. If he cannot bow, take off his cap, kiss his
hand, and say nothing, he has neither leg, hands, lip, nor cap,   10
and indeed such a fellow, to say precisely, were not made for
the court. But me, I got an answer, an answer for everything.

COUNTESS

That's an open-ended answer that fits all questions.

LAVATCH

It is like a barber's chair that fits all buttocks: small butt, big
butt, flat butt, juicy butt — or any buttock of any kind — oh   15
my god look at her butt.

COUNTESS

Will your answer serve to fit all questions?

LAVATCH

It fits good — real good — like money in the hands of a law-
yer, like a nail to its hole, like a scolding quean to a wran-
gling knave, like the nun's lip to the friar's mouth, no, like   20
the pudding to his skin. And if it fits that good, madam, you
better bag it up. One mustn't be too careful. Don't rush to put
the ring on a peasant's finger or give your French crown to a
common whore just because it will fit her. Cuz it will fit.

COUNTESS

I am asking do you have an answer for all questions?   25

LAVATCH

From below your duke to beneath your constable, it will fit
any question.

COUNTESS

It must be an answer of most monstrous size that must fit all
demands.

LAVATCH

Truth be told, it's a bit trifling — if the learn-ed should fess   30
up. I'm gonna give it to you straight. But first — let me strap
it on. Here it is, everything, all of it. Ask me if I am a courtier.
It shall do you no harm to learn.

COUNTESS

To be young again, if we could! I will be a fool in question,
hoping to be the wiser by your answer. I pray you, sir, are you   35
a courtier?

LAVATCH

Oh Lawd! My sweet Lord! — A simple answer. More, more,
ask me more — a hundred questions.

COUNTESS

Sir, I am a poor friend of yours that loves you.

LAVATCH

Oh Lawd! My sweet Lord! — Thick, thick. Lay it on me thick   40
— spare me not.

COUNTESS

I think, sir, you cannot handle it. You cannot eat this homely
meat. It may be old but it's still tender.

LAVATCH

Oh Lawd! My sweet Lord! Put me to it, I beg of you.

COUNTESS

I believe you were whipped recently, sir.   45

LAVATCH

Oh Lawd! My sweet Lord! Spare not me — Whoa, oh mercy
mercy me —

COUNTESS

Do you cry "Oh Lawd!" at your whipping, and "spare not
me"? Indeed, your "Oh Lord. My sweet Lord" sir is what you
might say at your whipping. You would have a good reply to   50
a good whipping, if you were bound up.

LAVATCH

I never had worse luck in my life with my "Oh Lawd! My sweet Lord!" I see things may serve long, but not forever.

Whoa mercy mercy mercy me

Ah things aren't what they use to be   55

COUNTESS

I play the noble housewife with the time,

To entertain it so merrily with a fool.

A fool like you.

LAVATCH

Oh Lawd! My sweet Lord! — Why, looky there — who knew

— it worked there too.   60

COUNTESS

An end, sir! To your business: Give this to Helen.

(*She gives him a letter. Pay attention. There are a lot of letters in this play.*)

And urge her to an instant answer back.

Give my regards to my kinsmen and my son.

This is not much.

LAVATCH

Your regards to them are not much?   65

COUNTESS

Not much for you to do I mean. You understand me?

LAVATCH

Most fruitfully. I am there before my legs.

COUNTESS

Hurry up then.

They exit in separate directions

ACT 2 ◆ SCENE 3

PARIS. THE KING'S PALACE.

Bertram, Lafeu, and Paroles enter

LAFEU

They say miracles are past, and we have our scientists to make things that seem supernatural and without cause quotidian and familiar. So then we make what once terrified us seem insignificant, ensconcing ourselves into what we think we know when what we should do is submit ourselves to the fear of the unknown. 5

PAROLES

Why, this is the greatest miracle of our times.

BERTRAM

And so it is.

LAFEU

To be relinquished by the physicians —

PAROLES

That's what I mean — both of Galen and Paracelsus. 10

LAFEU

Those two quacks? Of all the learned and authentic Fellows —

PAROLE

Right; that's what I mean.

LAFEU

They gave him up, incurable —

PAROLES

Why, yes, that's what I said too.

LAFEU

Not to be helped. 15

PAROLES

Right; as if he were a man assured of a —

LAFEU

Uncertain life and sure death.

PAROLES

That's it, that's exactly wht I would have said.

LAFEU

I must say it really is unusual.

PAROLES

It is indeed. If you want to see it in print, you shall read it in   20
what-do-you-call it. (*pointing to the ballad*)

LAFEU (*reading*)

"A showing of a heavenly effect in an earthly actor."

PAROLES

That's it, I would have said the very same.

LAFEU

Your sword is not shinier than mine. For me I speak with
respect —   25

PAROLES

No, it's strange, it's very strange. I mean the long and short of
it, and only a fiercely wicked man would refuse to acknowledge that it is the —

LAFEU

Very hand of heaven.

PAROLES

Yes. That's what I say.   30

LAFEU

In a most weak —

PAROLES

And weakly minister, great power, great transcendence,
which should indeed give us a further use to be made than
alone the recovery of the King as to be —

LAFEU

Generally thankful.   35

PAROLES

I would have said it, you say well. Here comes the King.

The King enters, healthy now, with his attendants and Helen, the one
that saved him, by his side. The mood of the court has shifted.
A celebration. The King leads Helen in a dance.

LAFEU

Lustily healthy. I'll too would like a maid better while I still
have all my teeth. Why, he's able to lead her in a dance.

PAROLES

Mon Dieu! Is that Helen?

LAFEU

By God, I think so. 40

KING

Go, call before me all the lords in court.

Sit, my life saver, by your patient's side,

(*the King and Helen sit*)

And with this healthy hand whose banished sense

You have repealed, a second time receive

The confirmation of my promised gift. 45

Just say the word. Who do you want?

Four Lords enter

Fair maid, send forth your eye. This youthful package

Of noble bachelors stand at my request,

O'er whom both sovereign power and father's voice

I have to use. Your frank selection make. 50

You have power to choose, they cannot forsake.

HELEN

To each of you a fair and virtuous maid

Fall when love please. Marry, except for one.

LAFEU (*aside*)

The horse's mouth is not yet broken in.

Oh what I'd give to be that young again 55

And have a little beard.

KING (*to Helen*)

    Peruse them well.

    Each one of them had a noble father.

HELEN

    Gentlemen,

    Through me, God has restored the King to health.   60

ALL FOUR LORDS

    We understand it, and thank God for you.

HELEN

    I am a simple maid, and therein wealthiest

    That I protest I simply am a maid.

    Please it your majesty, I have done already

    The blushes in my cheeks thus whisper me: 65

    "We blush that you should choose; but, if refused,

    Let the white virgin fever forever take you.

    We'll never come again."

KING

    Make choice, and see,

    Who shuns your love shuns all his love in me.   70

HELEN (*rising*)

    Now, Diane, from thy altar do I fly,

    And to imperial Love, that god most high,

    Do my sighs stream. (*to First Lord*) Sir, will you hear my suit?

FIRST LORD

    And grant it.

HELEN

    Thanks, sir. All the rest is mute.   75

LAFEU (*aside*)

    As sure as I'm alive, I would take my chance and play this
    game, though the dice seem loaded.

HELEN (*to Second Lord*)

    The honor, sir, that flames in your fair eyes,

Before I speak, too threat'ningly replies.
Love make your fortunes twenty times above   80
Her that so wishes, and her humble love.

SECOND LORD

No better, if you please.

HELEN

My wish receive,
Which great Love grant; and so I take my leave.

LAFEU (*aside*)

Do they all deny her? If they were sons of mine I'd have them   85
whipp'd.

HELEN (*to Third Lord*)

Be not afraid that I your hand should take;
I'll never do you wrong for your own sake.
Blessing upon your vows, and in your bed
Find fairer fortune, if you ever wed.   90

LAFEU (*aside*)

These boys are boys of ice, none of them will have her. They
must be the bastard sons of the English, the French are not
their fathers.

HELEN (*to Fourth Lord*)

You are too young, too happy, and too good
To give me a son — flesh of my own blood.   95

FOURTH LORD

Fair one, I think not so.

LAFEU (*aside*)

There's one grape yet: I am sure his father drunk wine, but
if he not an ass, I am a youth of fourteen; I have known him
already.

HELEN (*to Bertram*)

I dare not say I take you, but I give   100
Me and my service, ever while I live

Into your guiding power. — This is the man.

KING

Why then, young Bertram, take her, she's your wife.

BERTRAM

My wife, my liege? I beg of you, your highness

In matters like this — give me leave to use   105

The help of my own eyes.

KING

Do you not know

What she has done for me?

BERTRAM

Yes, my good lord,

But do not know why I should marry her.   110

KING

You know she raised me from my sickly bed.

BERTRAM

But does it follow, my lord, to bring me down

Because she raised you up? I know her well:

She had her breeding at my father's charge.

A poor physician's daughter, my wife?   115

I'd rather face your disdain than agree to this.

KING

It's only title you disdain in her, the which

I can build up. Strange is it that our bloods,

Of color, weight, and heat, pour'd all together,

Would quite confound distinction, yet stands off   120

In differences so mighty. If she be

All that is virtuous, save what you disliked —

"A poor physician's daughter" — you disliked

Of virtue for the name. But do not so.

From lowest place when virtuous things proceed,   125

The place is dignified by the doer's deed.

Where rank and status swells, and virtue none,
It is a diseased honor. Good alone
Is good, without a name. Vileness is so:
The property by what it is should go,   130
Not by the title. She is young, wise, fair.
In these to nature she's immediate heir,
And these breed honor; that is honor's scorn
Which challenges itself as honor's born
And is not like the sire; honor thrive   135
When rather from our acts we them derive
Than our foregoers. The mere word's a slave,
Deboshed on every tomb, on every grave
A lying trophy, and as oft is dumb,
Where dust and damned oblivion is the tomb   140
Of honored bones indeed. What should be said?
If you can't like this creature as a maid,
I can create the rest. Virtue and she
Is her own dower; honor and wealth from me.

BERTRAM

I cannot love her, nor will I strive to.   145

KING

You wrong yourself. If you should strive to choose —

HELEN

That you are well restored, my lord, I'm glad.
Let the rest go.

KING

My honor is at stake, which to defend,
I must produce my power. Here, take her hand,   150
Proud, scornful boy, unworthy this good gift,
That does in vile misprision shackle up
My love and her desert; that cannot dream
We, poising us in her defective scale,

Shall weigh you to the beam; that will not know   155
It is in us to plant your honor where
We please to have it grow. Check your contempt;
Obey our will, which travails for your good;
Believe not your disdain, but presently
Do your own fortunes that obedient right   160
Which both your duty owes and our power claims;
Or I will throw you from my care for ever
Into the staggers and the careless lapse
Of youth and ignorance, both my revenge and hate
Unleashing on you in the name of justice   165
Without all terms of pity. Speak. Your answer.

BERTRAM (*kneeling*)

Pardon, my gracious lord, for I submit
My fancy to your eyes. When I consider
What great creation and what dole of honor
Flies where you bid it, I find that she, which late   170
Was in my nobler thoughts most base, is now
The praised of the King; who, so ennobled,
As if she were born so.

KING

Take her by the hand
And tell her she is yours; to whom I promise   175
A counterweight to equal your estate
A balance most replete.

BERTRAM (*rising*)

I take her hand.

KING

Good fortune and the favor of the King
Smile upon this contract, whose ceremony   180
Shall seem expedient on the now-born brief,
And be perform'd at once. The solemn feast

45

Shall more attend upon the coming space,
Expecting absent friends. Your love to her
As sacred as your love to me.   185
Everything else is blasphemy.

> *Flourish. All exit but Paroles and Lafeu, who stay behind,*
> *commenting on this wedding.*

LAFEU

Do you hear that, monsieur? A word with you.

PAROLES

Your pleasure, sir.

LAFEU

Your lord and master did well to make his recantation.

PAROLES

Recantation? My lord? My master?   190

LAFEU

Yes. That's what I said. Do you not understand the language
I speak?

PAROLES

It is a most harsh one, and not to be understood without a
bloody fight. My master?

LAFEU

Are you companion to the Count Roussillon?   195

PAROLES

To any count, to all counts, to any man.

LAFEU

You are a count's man; but a count's master that's another story.

PAROLES

You are too old to fight, sir. Let it satisfy you, you are too old.

LAFEU

I must tell you, boy, I write "Man," to which title age cannot
bring you.   200

PAROLES

I dare not do what I want to do to you.

LAFEU

I did for a moment think you, for an ordinary person, to be
a pretty wise fellow. You did make the story of your travel
interesting enough. Yet the scarves and the bannerets about
you did in many ways dissuade me from believing you a ves- 205
sel of too great a burden. I have found you out, if I never see
you again I care not; some things are better lost than found.
Yet you are good for nothing but taking up and that you are
scarce worth.

PAROLES

Had you not the privilege of antiquity upon you — 210

LAFEU

Do not plunge yourself too far in anger, young buck, lest you
are ready to back it up. Lawd have mercy! Your taffeta scarf
wearing — I see right through you. Not even worth my time
so fare you well. — Boy, bye. Give me your hand. You might
want to keep it, as it is the high road. 215

PAROLES

My lord, you give me most egregious indignity.

LAFEU

Yes, with all my heart, and you are worthy of it.

PAROLES

I have not, my lord, deserved it.

LAFEU

Yes, good faith, every single ounce of it, and I have more to
give. 220

PAROLES

Well, I shall be the wiser.

LAFEU

Begin as soon as you can; for you must make up lost ground.

If ever you've been bound in your scarf and beaten you shall
find what it is to be proud of your bondage. I have a desire to
hold my acquaintance with you, or rather my knowledge of   225
you, so I can say I know exactly what you are like.

PAROLES

My lord, you do me most insupportable vexation.

LAFEU

For your sake, I wish, oh I wish, they were the pains of hell
and my poor doing eternal; I am beyond this, beyond you, in
what motion age will give me leave.   230

Lafeu exits. Paroles all alone.

PAROLES

Well, you have a son who shall take this disgrace off me.
Scurvy, old, filthy, scurvy lord. Well, I must be patient. There
is no fettering of authority. I'll beat him, by my life, when I
can meet him with any convenience, if he were double and
double a lord. I'll have no more pity of his age than I would   235
have of — I'll beat him, if I could but meet him again.

Lafeu re-enters. Paroles has his chance.

LAFEU

Servant, your lord and master's married. There's news for
you: You have a new mistress.

PAROLES

I most sincerely implore your lordship to make some reservation of your wrongs. He is my good lord, my patron; whom   240
I serve above is my master.

LAFEU

Who? God?

PAROLES

Yes, sir.

LAFEU

The devil is your master. Do other servants dress like you?

Make arms into legs by gartering them? If this is how you're   245
going to dress — flip-flop with no regard — do one better,
take what is between your legs, as it serves no purpose, and
wear it in place of your nose. By mine honor, if I were but two
hours younger I'd beat you. You are a general offence to man
and every man should beat you. I think you were created for   250
this very reason — so that men can unleash themselves upon
you.

PAROLES

This is hard and undeserved measure, my lord.

LAFEU

Stop, sir. You were beaten in Italy for picking a kernel out of
a pomegranate, you are a vagabond and no true traveler. You   255
are more saucy with lords and honorable personages than
the authority derived of your birth and virtue gives you the
right to. You are not worth another word, else I'd call you a
fool. I leave you.

Lafeu exits.

PAROLES

Good, very good, it is so then. Good, very good, let it lie awhile.   260

Bertram enters

BERTRAM

Undone and condemned to misery forever.

PAROLES

What's the matter, sweet bold fellow?

BERTRAM

Although before the solemn priest I have sworn, I will not
bed her.

PAROLES

What, what, dear boy?   265

BERTRAM

Oh my Paroles, they have married me.

I'll go to the Tuscan wars before I sleep with her.

PAROLES

France is a dog-hole, and it no more merits us being here
than the tread of a man's foot. To the wars!

BERTRAM

There's letters from my mother; what th' import is I don't 270
know yet.

PAROLES

So soon, we will find out. To th'wars, my boy, to th' wars!
He wears his honor in a box unseen
That hugs his erratic fancy here at home,
Spending his manly marrow in her arms, 275
Which should sustain the bound and high leap
Of Mars's fiery steed. To other regions!
France is a stable, we that dwell in it — jackasses.
Therefore to the war.

BERTRAM

It shall be so. I'll send her to my house, 280
Acquaint my mother with my hate for her,
And wherefore I am fled, write to the King
To which I dare not speak. His present gift
Shall furnish me to those Italian fields
Where noble fellows strike. Wars is no strife 285
To the dark house and the detested wife.

PAROLES

Are you sure this capriccio will hold?

BERTRAM

Go with me to my chamber and advise me.
I'll send her straight away. Tomorrow
To the wars I'll go, she to single sorrow. 290

PAROLES

You are the one in charge of this game now: 'Tis hard:

A young man married is a man that's marred.
Therefore away, and leave her bravely. Go.
The King has done you wrong, but hush it's so.

ACT 2 ◆ SCENE 4
PARIS. THE KING'S PALACE.
Helen and Lavatch enter.
He has a letter from the Countess. All's well.

HELEN

My mother sends me kind greetings. Is she well?

LAVATCH

She is not well, but yet she has her health. She's very merry
sure, but yet she is not well. But thanks be given she's very
well and wants nothing in this world. But yet she is not well.

HELEN

If she be very well, what ails her to make you say she is not   5
well?

LAVATCH

Truly, she's very well indeed, but for two things.

HELEN

What two things?

LAVATCH

One: she's not in heaven — may God send her there quickly.
The other: that she's still on earth — may God send her from   10
us quickly.

Paroles enters. He has news from Bertram.
It seems All's not so well after all.

PAROLES

Bless you, my fortunate lady.

HELEN

I hope, sir, I have your good will to have my own good fortunes.

PAROLES

You had my prayers to lead them on and to keep them on 15
have them still. — O my knave, how is my former lady?

LAVATCH

So that you had her wrinkles and I her money, I would she
did as you say.

PAROLES

Why, I say nothing.

LAVATCH

Well, you are the wiser man, for many a man's tongue shakes 20
out his master's undoing. To say nothing, do nothing, know
nothing, and to have nothing, is to be a great part of your
situation — empty words — basically amounts to nothing.

PAROLES

Away! You are a fool.

LAVATCH

You should have said, sir, "Before a fool, you are a fool" — 25
that is "Before me, you are a fool." This would be the truth,
sir.

PAROLES

Go away. I have found you out. You are a witty fool.

LAVATCH

Do you see me in yourself, sir, or were you taught to be like
me? 30

PAROLES

My own doing.

LAVATCH

The search, sir, was well worth it, and may you find the fool
in you, for the world's pleasure and the increase of laughter.

PAROLES

I think he's a good fool and well fed too.

(to Helen) Madam, my lord will go away tonight. 35

A very serious business calls on him.
He does acknowledge the great prerogative
And rite of love, which as your due, time claims.
But puts it off to a compelled restraint:
This unforseen delay is strewed with sweets,   40
Which will distill now in the curbed time,
To make the coming hour overflow with joy,
And pleasure drown the brim.

HELEN

What else does he wish?

PAROLES

That you will take your instant leave of the King,   45
And make this haste a choice of your own doing,
Strengthened with what apology you think
Will make it probable need.

HELEN

What more does he command?

PAROLES

That having this attained, you presently   50
Attend his further pleasure.

HELEN

In everything I wait upon his will.

PAROLES

I shall report it so.

HELEN

I pray you do.

Paroles exits

Come on, fool.   55

Helen and Lavatch exit

ACT 2 ◆ SCENE 5

PARIS. THE KING'S PALACE.

Lafeu talks smack to Bertram about Paroles

LAFEU

But I hope your lordship doesn't think he's a soldier.

BERTRAM

He is, my lord, and a proven valiant one.

LAFEU

How do you know this? Because he told you so?

BERTRAM

And so have others.

LAFEU

Then my radar must be off. I took this horse for an ass.   5

BERTRAM

I do assure you, my lord, he is very knowledgeable, and just
as valiant.

LAFEU

I have then sinned against his experience and transgressed
against his valor — and my state that way is irritating, since I
cannot yet find it in my heart to apologize. Here he comes. I   10
call on you to make us friends. I will make nice.

Paroles enters

PAROLES (*to Bertram*)

These things shall be done, sir.

LAFEU (*to Bertram*)

Dear God, sir, what is he wearing? Tell me who is his tailor?

PAROLES

Sir!

LAFEU

Sir is he. I know him well. Oh, "Sir," he "Sir" is a good work-   15
man, a very good tailor that can custom make a gentleman
from a common man.

BERTRAM (*aside to Paroles*)

Has she gone to the King?

PAROLES

She has.

BERTRAM

Will she go away tonight?   20

PAROLES

As you ordered.

BERTRAM

I have penned my letters, boxed up my treasures,

Given orders for our horses, and tonight,

When I should take possession of the bride,

I end before I begin.   25

LAFEU (*aside*)

A traveler's tale of his adventures is worth listening to towards the end of a good dinner, but one that lies a thousand times and uses a known truth to pass a thousand nothings with, should be once heard and thrice beaten. (*to Paroles*) God save you, captain.   30

BERTRAM (*to Paroles*)

Is there a problem between my lord and you, monsieur?

PAROLES

I don't know how I have deserved to run into my lord's displeasure.

LAFEU

And yet you run right into it — boots and spurs and all.

BERTRAM

It may be you have misunderstood him, my lord.   35

LAFEU

Fare you well, my lord, and you better write this down cuz I know it to be true. Eyes on the chalkboard I'll spell it out for you: There can be no kernel in this light nut. The soul of this

man is his clothes. Under all the scarves and gartered sleeves,
he is naked — has nothing, is nothing. He is an empty suit. Do 40
not trust him in matter of heavy consequence. I have tamed
men like him before, and I know their natures. — Farewell,
monsieur. I have spoken better of you than you have of me;
better than you deserve, but we must all do good against evil.

Lafeu exits

PAROLES

A trifling lord, I swear. 45

BERTRAM

I don't think so.

PAROLES

Why, don't you know him?

BERTRAM

Yes, I know him well; he's well-regarded.
And gets a pass. Here comes my wife.

Helen enters, attended

HELEN

I have, sir, as was commanded by you, 50
Spoke with the King, who granted his permission
To leave at once; only he desires
Some private speech with you.

BERTRAM

I shall obey his will.
You must not marvel, Ḥelen, at my course 55
Which holds not color with the time, nor does
Postpone my duty and required office
Of our contract. I was not prepared
For such a business, therefore I have found
So much unsettled. This drives me to entreat you 60
That presently you make your way for home,
And rather muse than ask why I entreat you,

For my reasons are better than they seem,
And my appointments have in them a need
Greater than shows itself at the first view   65
To you that know them not. Give this to my mother.

(*he gives her a letter*)

It will be two days before I see you,
I leave you to your own devices.

HELEN

Sir, I can say nothing
But that I am your most obedient servant.   70

She starts to cry

BERTRAM

Now, now, that's enough of that.

HELEN

And ever shall
With true observance seek to eek out that
Wherein toward me my homely stars have failed
To equal my great fortune.   75

BERTRAM

Let that go.
My haste is great. Farewell. So hurry home.

HELEN

Excuse me, sir.

BERTRAM

Well, what do you have to say?

HELEN

I am not worthy of the wealth I have,   80
Nor dare I say it's mine — and yet it is;
But like a timid thief, most meekly steal
What law does vouch my own.

BERTRAM

What would you have?

HELEN

> Something, and scarce so much: nothing indeed. 85
> I will not tell you what I want, my lord. Faith, yes:
> Only strangers and foes part and not kiss.

BERTRAM

> I'm telling you, stay not but haste to horse.

HELEN

> I shall not break your bidding, good my lord. —
> Where are my other men? — Monsieur, farewell. 90

Helen exits, with attendants

BERTRAM

> Go you toward home, where I will never come
> As long as I can shake my sword or hear the drum.
> We steal away tonight.

PAROLES

> Bravely. Coraggio!

They exit

ACT 3 ♦ SCENE 1
FLORENCE. THE DUKE'S PALACE.

Flourish of trumpets. Enter the Duke of Florence and the two Lords
Dumaine, with a troop of soldiers. The men talk about war and
I wonder would there still be war if there were no men?

DUKE

And so from point to point now you have heard
The fundamental reasons of this war,
The great decision has let forth much blood,
And thirsts for more.

1 DUMAINE

The quarrel seems holy   5
Upon your grace's part; dark and fearful
On the part of the opponent.

DUKE

That's why we marvel that our cousin France
Would in so just a business shut his heart
Against our borrowing prayers.   10

1 DUMAINE

My good lord,
The reasons of our state I cannot yield
And like a common and an outward man
I can only guess why the council makes
The decisions that they do; I dare not   15
Say what I think of it, since I have found
Myself in my uncertain grounds to fail
As often as I guess'd.

DUKE

He will do what he thinks is right.

1 DUMAINE

But I am sure the younger of our country,   20

That surfiet on their ease will day by day

Come here for some relief.

DUKE

They will be welcome,

And all the honors that can fly from us

Will settle on them. You know your places well;   25

When better fall, they fall for your advance.

Tomorrow to the field.

They exit

ACT 3 ◆ SCENE 2

ROUSILLON. THE COUNT'S PALACE.

The Countess enters with Lavatch following behind her

COUNTESS

It has all happened as I would have wanted it to, except that he is not coming along with her.

LAVATCH

I swear, I take my young lord to be a very sad, sad man.

Lavatch hands her Bertram's letter

COUNTESS

Might I ask why you would say that?

LAVATCH

Why, he will look upon his boot and sing; adjust his collar   5
and sing; ask questions and sing; pick his teeth and sing. I know a man as sad as him who sold a goodly manor for a song.

COUNTESS

Let me see what he writes, and when he means to come. (*reads the letter*)

LAVATCH (*aside*)

Isbel has not been on my mind since I was at court. The   10
brains of my Cupid's been rattled, and I begin to love as an
old man loves money: without appetite.

COUNTESS

What have we here?

LAVATCH

What you have there.

Lavatch exits

COUNTESS (*reads the letter aloud*)

"I have sent you a daughter-in-law. She has saved the King   15
and ruined me. I have wedded her, not bedded her, and
sworn to make the 'not' eternal. You will hear that I have
run away; I wanted you to hear it from me first. If there be
enough distance in the world I will stay far away. My duty to
you. Your unfortunate son, Bertram."   20

This is not well, rash and hardheaded boy,

To fly the favors of so good a King,

To pluck his indignation on your head

By the misprizing of a maid too virtuous

For the contempt of empire.   25

Lavatch re-enters

LAVATCH

O madam, there is bad news over there, between two soldiers
and my young lady.

COUNTESS

What is the matter?

LAVATCH

Well, there is some comfort in the news, some comfort. Your
son will not be killed as soon as I thought he would.   30

COUNTESS

Why should he be killed?

LAVATCH

So say I, madam — if he run away, as I hear he has, the danger is in standing up; that's what brings good men down. Here they come and will tell you more. For my part, I only heard your son has run away.   35

Lavatch exits

Helen enters with another letter, and the two Lords Dumaine

HELEN

Madam, my lord is gone, for ever gone.

COUNTESS (*to Helen*)

Have patience, Helen. — Please, gentlemen,

I don't know what to believe.

I have felt so many quirks of joy and grief   40

That I am about to break down under

The weight of it all. Please tell me, where is my son?

2 DUMAINE

Madam, he's gone to serve the Duke of Florence.

We met him on his way, from there we came,

And, after we dispatch some news at court,   45

We will return again.

HELEN

Look at his letter: my walking papers.

(*reads aloud*) "When you can get the ring upon my finger, which never shall come off, and show me a child begotten of your body that I am father to, then call me husband; but in   50
such a 'then' I write a 'never.'"

This is a dreadful sentence.

COUNTESS

Brought you this letter, gentlemen?

1 DUMAINE

Yes, madam,

And for the contents' sake are sorry for our pains.   55

COUNTESS

    I beg you, Helen, have a better cheer.

    If you would pile up all the griefs as yours

    You rob me of my share. He was my son,

    But I do wash his name out of my blood,

    Now you are all my child. To Florence, is he?   60

2 DUMAINE

    Yes, madam.

COUNTESS

    And to be a soldier?

2 DUMAINE

    That is his noble purpose, and — believe it —

    The Duke will lay upon him all the honor

    That his nobility claims.   65

COUNTESS

    Return you there?

1 DUMAINE

    Yes, madam, with the swiftest wing of speed.

HELEN

    "Until I have no wife, I have nothing in France."

    That's bitter.

COUNTESS

    That's what it says?   70

HELEN

    Yes, madam.

1 DUMAINE

    It's just the boldness of his hand, perhaps, which his heart

    was not consenting to.

COUNTESS

    Nothing in France until he have no wife?

    There is nothing here that is too good for him   75

    But only she, and she deserves a lord

That twenty such rude boys might tend upon
And call her, hourly, mistress. Who was with him?

1 DUMAINE

Only a retainer, a gentleman
Whom I have met before. 80

COUNTESS

Paroles, was it not?

1 DUMAINE

Yes, my good lady, him.

COUNTESS

A very tainted fellow, and full of wickedness.
My son corrupts a well-derived nature
With his incentive. 85

1 DUMAINE

Indeed, good lady,
The fellow has a deal of that too much,
It serves to his advantage.

COUNTESS

You're welcome, gentlemen.
I will ask you, when next you see my son, 90
To tell him that his sword can never win
The honor that he loses; more I'll write
For you to bear to him.

2 DUMAINE

We serve you, madam,
In this and all your worthiest affairs. 95

COUNTESS

Not so, but as we exchange courtesies.
Will you come with me?

All but Helen exit

HELEN

"Until I have no wife I have nothing in France."

Nothing in France until he has no wife.
You shall have none, Roussillon, none in France;   100
Then have you all again. Poor lord, is't I
That chases you from your country and exposes
Those tender limbs of yours to the event
Of the none-sparing war? And is it I
That drives you from the sportive court, where you   105
Were shot at with fair eyes, to be the mark
Of smoky muskets? O you leaden messengers
That ride upon the violent speed of fire,
Fly with false aim, cleave the still-piecing air
That sings with piercing, do not touch my lord.   110
Whoever shoots at him, I put him there.
Whoever charges at his forward breast,
I am the coward that holds him to it,
And though I kill him not, I am the cause
Of his effected death. It would be better   115
I met the rav'nous lion when he roared
With sharp constraint of hunger; better it were
That all the miseries which nature owes
Were mine at once. No, you come home, Roussillon,
Where honor except of risk wins a scar,   120
As often lost as gained. I will be gone;
My being here it is that holds you hence.
Shall I stay here to do't? No, no, although
The air of paradise did fan the house
And angels performed all services. I will be gone,   125
So pitiful rumors may report my flight
And so console your ear. Come night, end day;
And with the dark, poor thief, I'll steal away.

Helen exits

ACT 3 ♦ SCENE 3
FLORENCE

Flourish of trumpets. The Duke of Florence and Bertram enter,
with drummer and trumpeters, soldiers, and Paroles.

DUKE (*to Bertram*)

    You are the general of our horse, and we,

    Filled with our hope, lay our best love and faith

    Upon your promising fortune.

BERTRAM

    Sir, it is

    A charge too heavy for my strength, and yet   5

    We'll strive to bear it for your worthy sake

    To the extreme edge of hazard.

DUKE

    Then go forth,

    And may Fortune dance upon your prosperous helm

    As your auspicious mistress.   10

BERTRAM

    Great God of War

    This very day, I give myself to you.

    Take me for my word, and I'll prove myself

    A lover of your drum, hater of love.

They exit

ACT 3 ♦ SCENE 4
ROUSILLON. THE COUNT'S PALACE.

The Countess and Reynaldo enter, with a letter from Helen

COUNTESS

    Oh! Why would you take the letter from her?

    Did you not know she would do what she has done,

    By sending me a letter? Read it again.

REYNALDO (*reads*)

"I'm on a pilgrimage to Saint Jaques'.
Because my ambitious love has offended,
I plod upon the cold ground on barefoot,
Asking the saint to rectify my faults
Write, write, that my dearest master, your dear son,
May return from the bloody course of war.   5
Bless him at home in peace, while I from far
Will sanctify his name with zealous fervor.
Ask that he forgive me for what I have taken;
I, his despiteful Juno, sent him forth
From courtly friends, with camping foes to live,   10
Where death and danger dogs the heels of worth.
He is too good and fair for death and me;
Whom I myself embrace to set him free."

COUNTESS

Oh, what sharp stings are in her mildest words!
Reynaldo, you did never lack advice so much   15
As letting her go so. Had I spoke with her,
I could have well diverted her intents,
But she has prevented that.

REYNALDO

I'm sorry, madam.
If I had given this to you last night   20
She might have been overtaken — but she adds
Pursuit would be in vain.

COUNTESS

What angel would
Bless this unworthy husband? He cannot thrive
Unless her prayers, whom heaven delights to hear   25
And loves to grant, reprieve him from the wrath
Of greatest justice. Write, write, Reynaldo,

To this unworthy husband of his wife.
Let every word weigh heavy of her worth,
That he does weigh too light; my greatest grief, 30
Though little does he feel it, set down sharply.
Dispatch the most expedient messenger.
When time comes he shall hear that she is gone,
He will return, and I hope may that she,
Hearing of his return, will speed back here, 35
Led solely by pure love. Which of them both
Is dearest to me, I have no skill in sense
To make distinction. Get this messenger.
My heart is heavy and mine age is weak;
Grief would have tears, and sorrow bids me speak. 40

They exit

ACT 3 ♦ SCENE 5

OUTSIDE FLORENCE

A series of notes on the trumpet in the distance.
Widow Capilet, her daughter Diana, and Mariana enter,
with other Florentine citizens.

WIDOW

No, come; because if they do approach the city, we shall lose
all sight of them.

DIANA

They say the French Count has done most honorable service.

WIDOW

It is reported that he has captured their best commander, and
that he slew the Duke's brother with his own hands. 5

(*trumpets sound a call to the cavalry*)

All our work for naught; they have gone a different way. You
may know by their trumpets.

MARIANA

Come, let's go back and be content with the report of it. —
Well, Diana, take heed of this French count. The honor of a
maid is her name, and no legacy is so rich as chastity. 10

WIDOW (*to Diana*)

I have told my neighbor how you have been solicited by a
gentleman, his companion.

MARIANA

I know that fool, hang him! His name is Paroles; a filthy officer pandering for the young Count. Beware of them, Diana;
their promises, enticements, oaths, tokens, and all their 15
engines of lust, are nothing more than a masquerade. Many a
virgin has been seduced by them; they will steal your virginity and do not care the misery they leave in the wreckage of
maidenhood. I hope I do not need to advise you further, but
I hope your own grace will keep you where you are, though 20
there were no further danger known but the modesty which
is so lost.

DIANA

You do not need to fear for me.

Helen enters dressed as a pilgrim

WIDOW

I hope so. Look, here comes a pilgrim. I know she will stay at
my house; because they send one another here. I'll question 25
her. God save you, pilgrim. Where are you going?

HELEN

To Saint Jaques le Grand.

Where do the pilgrims stay, can you tell me?

WIDOW

At the "Saint Francis" here next to the port.

HELEN

Is this the way? 30

69

WIDOW

Yes, in fact, it is.

(*sound of a march, far off*)

Listen, they come this way. If you will wait,
Holy pilgrim, until the troops come by,
I will conduct you to where you will stay,
The sooner for I think I know your hostess   35
As well as I do myself.

HELEN

Is it you?

WIDOW

If you wish it, yes, pilgrim.

HELEN

I thank you, and will stay upon your leisure.

WIDOW

You came from France, I think?   40

HELEN

I did.

WIDOW

Here you will see a countryman of yours
That has done worthy service.

HELEN

May I ask his name?

DIANA

The Count Roussillon. Do you know him?   45

HELEN

Only by ear, that hears most nobly of him;
I do not know his face.

DIANA

Whoever he is,
He's bravely thought of here. He fled from France,
As is reported; because the King had married him   50

Against his liking. Do you think this is true?

HELEN

Oh yes, absolutely true. I know his wife.

DIANA

There is a gentleman that serves the Count

Reports most coarsely of her.

HELEN

What's his name?   55

DIANA

Monsieur Paroles.

HELEN

Oh, I agree with him,

Comparing her in praise or to the worth

Of the great Count himself, she is too humble

To have her name repeated. All she has   60

Is her carefully guarded chastity,

And that, I've never heard questioned.

DIANA

Oh, poor lady.

It's a hard bondage to become the wife

Of a detesting lord.   65

WIDOW

I'm sure, good creature, wherever she is,

Her heart weighs sadly. This young maid might do her

A shrewd turn if she pleased.

HELEN

What do you mean?

Maybe the amorous Count solicits her   70

In the unlawful purpose.

WIDOW

He does indeed,

And tries everything he can to

Corrupt the tender honor of this maid.
But she is armed and ready, and keeps her guard 75
In the most honest defense against him.

MARIANA

Heaven forbid!

Bertram and Paroles enter with drummer,
colors, and the whole army

WIDOW

So, here they come:
That is Antonio, the Duke's eldest son;
That Escalus. 80

HELEN

Which is the Frenchman?

DIANA

He —
The one with the plume. The most gallant fellow.
If only he loved his wife. If he were more honest
He might be as good. Isn't he 85
A handsome gentleman?

HELEN

I like him well.

DIANA

Too bad he is not honest.
And there's that fool that leads him to these places.
If I were his woman, I would poison 90
That vile rascal.

HELEN

Which one is he?

DIANA

That jackanapes with scarves. Why is he melancholy?

HELEN

Maybe he was hurt in the battle.

PAROLES (*aside*)

Lose our drum? Well.   95

MARIANA

He's certainly upset about something. Look, he has seen us.

WIDOW (*to Paroles*)

Marry, hang you!

Paroles bows

MARIANA (*to Paroles*)

And your curtesy, for a go between.

Bertram, Paroles, and the army exit

WIDOW

The troops are gone. Come, pilgrim, I will take you

To your lodgings. There are some four or five   100

Devout penitants bound to Saint Jaques

Already at my house.

HELEN

I humbly thank you.

Please it this matron and this gentle maid

To dine with us tonight; the charge and thanking   105

Shall be on me, and, to requite you further,

I will tell you some things this virgin knows bestow

Worthy the note.

DIANA AND MARIANA

We'll take your kindly offer.

They exit

ACT 3 ◆ SCENE 6

THE FLORENTINE CAMP

Bertram enters with the two Captains Dumaine

1 DUMAINE (*to Bertram*)

No, my good lord, put him to it. Put him to the test and he
will show you his true colors.

2 DUMAINE (*to Bertram*)

I bet my reputation on it, my lordship. He is nothing but a good for nothing

1 DUMAINE (*to Bertram*)

On my life, my lord, he is all show.

BERTRAM

Do you think that he has me completely fooled?

1 DUMAINE

Believe it, my lord. I've seen it with my own eyes — without any malice, but to speak of him as my kinsman — he's a most notable coward, an infinite and endless liar, an hourly prom-   5
ise-breaker, the owner of no one good quality worthy of your lordship's entertainment.

1 DUMAINE (*to Bertram*)

It's only fitting that you know exactly who he is, so that you do not put your trust in him because he is not to be trusted. He is not a man of virtue or courage. And when you most   10
need him, in a moment of danger, he will fail you. Trust.

BERTRAM

I wish I knew how I could test him.

2 DUMAINE

None better than to let him rescue his drum, which you hear him so confidently undertake to do.

1 DUMAINE (*to Bertram*)

I will surprise him suddenly with a troop of Florentines.   15
I will have with me men I am sure he knows not from the enemy; we will bind and blindfold him so, that he will think that he is being carried into the military camp of the adver-saries when we bring him to our own tents. All you have to do, my lordship, is be present at this test: if he does not offer   20
to betray you and deliver all the intelligence in his power against you, in exchange for the promise of his life and in the

highest compulsion of base fear, swearing his very soul on
their truths, never trust my judgment in anything ever again.

2 DUMAINE (*to Bertram*)

Oh, just for fun, let him fetch his drum. He says he has a   25
strategy for it. When your lordship sees where this is going,
and to what metal this counterfeit lump of ore will be melted,
if you don't go along with this game, you will always doubt
yourself. Here he comes.

Paroles enters

1 DUMAINE

Oh (*aside*) just for fun (*aloud*) do not get in the way of his   30
plans; in any case, let him fetch his drum.

BERTRAM (*to Paroles*)

How now, monsieur? This drum sticks sorely in your dispo-
sition.

2 DUMAINE

Curse the drum, let it go. It's just a drum.

PAROLES

Just a drum? Is it just a drum? A drum so lost! There was   35
excellent command: to charge in with our horse upon our
own wings and to violently rip our own soldiers into pieces!

2 DUMAINE

You can't blame that on command. It was a disaster of war
that Caesar himself could not have prevented, if he himself
had been there to command.   40

BERTRAM

Well, we cannot greatly condemn our success. There was
some dishonor in the loss of that drum, but it will not be
recovered.

PAROLES

We could have recovered it.

BERTRAM

Could of, should of, would of, but we didn't.   45

PAROLES

It will be recovered. But that the merit of service is seldom
attributed to the true and exact performer, I will fetch that
drum or any another. I bet my life on it.

BERTRAM

Why, if you are hungry for it, get to it, monsieur. If you think
your skill in stratagem can bring this instrument of honor   50
again into its native quarter, be magnanimous in the enter-
prise and go on. I will grace the attempt for a worthy exploit.
If you do what you do swiftly and well, the Duke shall both
speak of it and extend to you what further becomes his great-
ness, even to the utmost syllable of your worthiness.   55

PAROLES

By the hand of a soldier, I will undertake this challenge.

BERTRAM

But you must not sleep on it.

PAROLES

I'll be about it this evening, but not before I write out a list
of all my challenges, encourage myself in my knowing, put
myself into my mortal preparation; by midnight look to hear   60
further from me.

BERTRAM

May I be bold to tell his grace what you are doing?

PAROLES

I don't know how successful I will be, my lord, but I vow to
make every attempt.

BERTRAM

I know you are valiant, and your soldiership will attest for   65
you. Farewell.

PAROLES

I am not a man of many words.

Paroles exits

1 DUMAINE

No more than a fish loves water. (*to Bertram*) Isn't he a strange fellow, my lord, that he so confidently seems to undertake this business, which he knows can't be done? Damns himself 70 to do it, and dares better be damned than to do it.

2 DUMAINE (*to Bertram*)

You do not know him, my lord, like we do. Certain it is that he will steal himself into a man's favor, and for a week escape a great deal of discoveries, but when you find him out, you have him ever after. 75

BERTRAM

What, do you think he will make no attempt at all of this that so seriously he has been promising?

1 DUMAINE

Not a chance in the world, but he will come back with a story, and foist upon you two or three probable lies. But we have almost ensnared him. You will see him go down tonight; 80 because indeed he is not worthy of your lordship's respect.

2 DUMAINE (*to Bertram*)

The old Lord Lafeu first sniffed him out. We'll have some fun with the young fox before we skin him of his disguise; you will see he's nothing but a moppet, and you will see this tonight. 85

1 DUMAINE

Let me set my traps. He will be caught.

BERTRAM

Your brother will go along with me.

1 DUMAINE

As it pleases your lordship. I'll leave you.

1 Dumaine exits

BERTRAM

Now I will take you to the house, and show you the girl I
spoke of.   90

2 DUMAINE

But you say she's honest.

BERTRAM

That is the thing. I spoke with her but once
And found her ice cold, but have sent to her
Tokens and letters, which she then returned,
And this is all I have done. She's a fair creature.   95
Will you go with me to see her?

2 DUMAINE

Of course, my lord.

They exit

ACT 3 ◆ SCENE 7

FLORENCE. THE WIDOW'S HOUSE.

Helen and the Widow enter

HELEN

If you misdoubt me that I am not she,
I don't know how else to assure you further
But I know we will lose grounds on my plan.

WIDOW

Though my estate has fallen, I was well-born.
I do not deal in shady businesses,   5
And would not put my reputation now
Through any staining act.

HELEN

Nor would I want you to.
First believe that the Count he is my husband,

And what to your sworn counsel I have spoken   10
Is true from word to word, and then you cannot,
By the good aid that I will borrow of you.
Err in bestowing it.

WIDOW

I should believe you,
For you have show'd me that which surely proves   15
You're great in fortune.

HELEN

Take this purse of gold,
And let me buy your friendly help so far,
Which I will over-pay and pay again
When you help me more. The Count woos your daughter,   20
Lays down his wanton siege before her beauty,
He wants her. Let her give him what he wants,
And we'll direct her how best to do that.
Now his persistent lust will not deny
What she'll demand: a ring worn by the Count,   25
Which has been handed down in succession
From son to son some four or five descents
Since the first father wore it. This ring he holds
Most dear to him; yet, in his idle fire,
To win his prize it would not seem too dear.   30
Even if he regrets it afterwards.

WIDOW

Now I see the substance of your purpose.

HELEN

You see it lawful then. It is no more
But that your daughter seeming to give in,
Asks for the ring; and sets up the meeting;   35
In time, I will be there to take her place,

Herself most chastely absent. After,
To her dowry I'll add three thousand crowns
To what has already been paid.   40

WIDOW

I agree to it.
Tell my daughter how and what she should do,
The time and place with this deceit so lawful
May prove coherent. Every night he comes
With musics of all sorts, and songs composed   45
To her unworthiness. It doesn't matter
If we tell him not to, for he persists
As if his life depends on it.

HELEN

Tonight
Let us try out our plan, which, if it speed   50
Is wicked meaning in a lawful deed
And lawful meaning in a wicked act,
Though neither sinful, still a sinful fact.
So let's get to it.

They exit

ACT 4 ◆ SCENE 1

OUTSIDE THE FLORENTINE CAMP

1 Dumaine enters, with five or six other soldiers, in an ambush

1 DUMAINE

He can only come by the corner of this hedge. When you come up on him, speak what fearsome nonsense language you want. It won't matter that you don't understand, what matters is that we seem not to understand him, except for one person among us, whom we must produce for an inter- 5 preter.

INTERPRETER (FIRST SOLDIER)

Good captain, let me be the interpreter.

1 DUMAINE

Are you acquainted with him? Does he know your voice?

INTERPRETER.

No, sir, I promise you. He does not.

1 DUMAINE

But what mumbo jumbo will you use to reply to us? 10

INTERPRETER.

The same that you speak to me.

1 DUMAINE

He must think us some group of strangers employed by the enemy. Now he knows a bit of all the neighboring languages, therefore everybody must talk their own made up language; as long as we seem to understand each other, we get what we 15 want — talk-talk, wiri-wiri, talk-talk. As for you, interpreter, you must seem very politic. But lie low, ho! Here he comes, to get two hours in of sleep, before he goes back to swear on the lies he tells.

They hide. Paroles enters. Clock strikes.

PAROLES

Ten o'clock. Within these three hours it will be time for me   20
to go home. What shall I say I have done? It must be a very
plausible invention that carries it. They begin to smoke me
out, and disgraces have knocked too often at my door of late.
I find my tongue fast and loose, but in my heart I am afraid of
war, and the warlike noises of my boasting tongue.   25

1 DUMAINE (*aside*)

This is the first truth that your own tongue was ever guilty of.

PAROLES

What the devil should move me to undertake the recovery
of this drum, knowing it is impossible, and knowing I had
no such intent? I must hurt myself in some way, and say I
got injured in exploit. Yet they can't be minor injuries. They   30
will say, "Came you off with so little?" And great ones I dare
not give. So, what's the instance? Tongue, I must put you into
a gossip's mouth, and buy myself another mute mule, if you
keep on and on putting me into these perils.

1 DUMAINE (*aside*)

Is it possible he could know what he is, and still be that way?   35

PAROLES

I wish the cutting of my garments would serve the turn, or
the breaking of my Spanish sword.

1 DUMAINE (*aside*)

We cannot allow you to.

PAROLES

Or I could shave my beard, and say it was part of my strategy.

1 DUMAINE (*aside*)

That won't trick us.   40

PAROLES

Or I could drown my clothes, and say I was stripped.

1 DUMAINE (*aside*)

Hardly serve.

PAROLES

Even if I swore I leapt from the window of the fortress?

1 DUMAINE (*aside*)

How high?

PAROLES

180 feet.   45

1 DUMAINE (*aside*)

Swear it three times and it would still seem unbelievable.

PAROLES

I wish I had a drum, any drum, of the enemy's. I would swear
I recovered it.

1 DUMAINE (*aside*)

You shall hear one soon enough.

PAROLES

A drum now of the enemy's —   50

Sound of a drum. The ambush rushes in.

1 DUMAINE

Tikka masala, eres bien mala.

SOLDIERS

Wop, wop, wop, wop, wop.

They seize and blindfold him

PAROLES

Oh kidnap, kidnap, do not hide mine eyes.

They blindfold him

INTERPRETER

Boskos thromuldo boskos.

PAROLES

I know you are the Moscow's regiment,   55
And I shall lose my life for lack of language.
If there be here German or Dane, Low Dutch,

Italian, or French, if he speaks to me,
I'll reveal that which will undo the Florentine.

INTERPRETER

Boskos vauvado. — 60

I understand you, and can speak your tongue. — Kerely-
bonto. —

Sir, I suggest you pray, because seventeen daggers are pointed
at your chest.

PAROLES

Oh! 65

INTERPRETER

Oh pray, pray, pray! —

Manka Ivanka Dolce Gabbana?

1 DUMAINE

Oscorbidulchos volivorco.

INTERPRETER

The general is content to spare you yet,
And, blindfolded as you are, will lead you on 70
To gather from you. Perhaps you may reveal
Something to save your life.

PAROLES

Oh let me live,
And I'll share all the secrets of our camp,
Their force, their purposes; more, I'll speak that 75
Which you will marvel at.

INTERPRETER

But will you do so in good faith?

PAROLES

If I do not, damn me.

INTERPRETER

Acordo linta. —

Come on, you are granted pause. 80

ACT 4 ◆ SCENE 1

Sound of drums

They exit all but 1 Dumaine and Second Soldier

1 DUMAINE

Go tell the Count Roussillon and my brother

We have caught the peacock, and will keep him muffled

Until we hear from them.

SECOND SOLDIER

Captain, I will.

1 DUMAINE

And he will betray us all unto ourselves.   85

Inform them that.

SECOND SOLDIER

So I will, sir.

1 DUMAINE

Until then I will keep him safely locked.

They exit

ACT 4 ◆ SCENE 2

FLORENCE. THE WIDOW'S HOUSE.

Bertram and the maid Diana enter

BERTRAM

They told me that your name was Fontibel.

DIANA

No, my good lord, Diana.

BERTRAM

Named for a goddess,

Well-deserved and then some. But, fair soul,

In your fine frame does love have no value?   5

If the quick fire of youth lights not your mind,

You are no maiden but a monument.

When you are dead you should be such a one

As you are now, for you are cold and stern,

Instead you should be as your mother was   10
When your sweet self was conceived.

DIANA

She was honest then.

BERTRAM

You should be too.

DIANA

No.
My mother did her duty; such, my lord,   15
As you owe to your wife.

BERTRAM

No more of that.
Please, do not make me go against my vows.
I was forced to wed her, but I love you
By love's own sweet constraint, and will for ever   20
Serve you as a lover would.

DIANA

Yes, so you serve us
Till we serve you; but when you have our roses,
You barely leave our thorns to prick ourselves,
And mock us with our bareness.   25

BERTRAM

But I have sworn!

DIANA

It's not the many oaths that makes the truth,
But the plain single vow you vow to keep.
We do not swear by that which is not holy,
But ask the highest to witness; then pray you, tell me,   30
If I should swear by Jove's great attributes
I loved you dearly, would you believe my oaths
When I did love you not? This has no holding,
To swear by God whom I protest to love

That I will work against Him. Therefore your oaths   35
Are words and poor conditions but unsealed,
At least in my opinion.

BERTRAM

Change it, change it.
Do not be so holy-cruel. Love is holy,
And my integrity never knew the crafts   40
That you do charge men with. Stand off no more,
But give yourself unto my sick desires,
So I'll recover. Say you are mine, and ever
My love as it begins shall so persevere.

DIANA

I see that men tie ropes in knots so tight   45
That we'll give up ourselves. Give me that ring.

BERTRAM

I'll lend you it, my dear, but have no power
To give it to you.

DIANA

Will you not, my lord?

BERTRAM

It is an honor 'longing to our house,   50
Bequeathed down from many ancestors,
Which would invite the greatest condemnation
For me to lose.

DIANA

My honor's such a ring.
My chastity's the jewel of our house,   55
Bequeathed down from many ancestors,
Which would invite the greatest condemnation
For me to lose. Thus your own proper wisdom
Calls for my champion Honor to protect me
Against your vain assault.   60

BERTRAM

Here, take my ring.

My house, my honor, yes my life be yours,

And I will do as you command.

DIANA

When midnight comes, knock at my chamber window.

I'll see to it my mother shall not hear.   65

Now I will charge you in the bond of truth,

When you have conquered my yet maiden bed,

Remain there for an hour, nor speak to me —

My reasons are most strong, and you will know them

When back again this ring shall be delivered —   70

And on your finger in the night I'll put

Another ring that, what in time proceeds,

May token to the future our past deeds.

Adieu till then; then, fail not. You have won

A wife of me, though there my hope be done.   75

BERTRAM

A heaven on earth I have won by wooing you.

DIANA

May you live long to thank both heaven and me.

You may so in the end.

Bertram exits

My mother told me just how he would woo me,

As if she sat in his heart. She says all men   80

Spit the same game. He has sworn to marry me

When his wife's dead; I'll sleep with him over

My dead body. Since Frenchmen, I'm afraid,

Marry at will, I will live and die a maid.

Only, in this disguise I think it's no sin   85

To mislead him that would unjustly win.

Diana exits

ACT 4 ◆ SCENE 3
THE FLORENTINE CAMP
The two Captains Dumaine enter with some two or three soldiers

1 DUMAINE

You have not given him his mother's letter?

2 DUMAINE

I delivered it an hour ago. There is something in it that stings his nature, for on the reading it he changed almost into another man.

1 DUMAINE

He has much deserved blame laid upon him for shaking off 5 so good a wife and so sweet a lady.

2 DUMAINE

He has especially incurred the everlasting displeasure of the King, who had fully tuned his bounty to sing happiness to him. I will tell you something, but you have to promise to keep it under lock and key. 10

1 DUMAINE

I will take it to my grave.

2 DUMAINE

He has perverted a young gentlewoman here in Florence of a most chaste reputation, and tonight he fleshes his will in the spoil of her honor. He has given her his family ring, and thinks he made out like a bandit in this extramarital contract. 15

1 DUMAINE

God, delay our rebellion of the flesh! As we are ourselves, what things are we.

2 DUMAINE

We are traitors to ourselves. And as in the common course of all treasons we still see them reveal themselves until they attain their abhorrent ends, by doing so he goes against his 20 own nobility, in this polluted stream drowns himself.

1 DUMAINE

Is it not meant damnable in us to be trumpeters of our unlawful intents? So we will not have his company tonight?

2 DUMAINE

Not until after midnight.

1 DUMAINE

Midnight will soon be here. I would gladly have him see his 25 company anatomized, that he might take a measure of his own judgements, wherein so richly he had set this counter-feit.

2 DUMAINE

We will not meddle with him until he comes, for his presence must be the whip of the other. 30

1 DUMAINE

In the meantime, what do you hear of these wars?

2 DUMAINE

I hear there is an overture of peace.

1 DUMAINE

No, I assure you, a peace concluded.

2 DUMAINE

What will Count Roussillon do now? Will he continue to travel, or return again to France? 35

1 DUMAINE

I can see by your questions that you are not altogether a part of his council.

2 DUMAINE

Let it be forbid, sir; so should I be a great deal of his act.

1 DUMAINE

Sir, his wife fled from his house some two months ago. Her pretense a pilgrimage to Saint Jaques le Grand, which holy 40 undertaking with most austere sanctimony she accom-plished, and there residing, the tenderness of her nature became as a prey to her grief: at last, she made a groan of her last breath, and now she sings in heaven.

2 DUMAINE

How do you know this to be true?   45

1 DUMAINE

By her own letters, which makes her story true even to the point of her death. Her death itself, she could not report, but it was faithfully confirmed by the rector of the place.

2 DUMAINE

Does the Count know about this?

1 DUMAINE

Yes, and the particular confirmations, point from point, to   50
the full arming of the verity.

2 DUMAINE

I am truly sorry that he'll be glad about this.

1 DUMAINE

How mightily sometimes we find comfort in our losses.

2 DUMAINE

And how mightily some other times we drown our gain in tears. The great dignity that his valor has here acquired for   55
him shall at home be encountered with a shame as ample.

1 DUMAINE

The web of our life is of a mingled yarn, good and bad together. We would be proud of our virtues if it weren't for our faults, and our crimes would despair if they were not cherished by our virtues.   60

A Messenger enters

How now? Where's your master?

MESSENGER

He met the Duke in the street, sir, where he said his good-byes. His lordship will go to France in the morning. The Duke has offered him letters of commendations to the King.

Messenger exits

2 DUMAINE

They will not be enough.   65

Bertram enters

1 DUMAINE

They cannot be too sweet for the King's tartness. Here's his lordship now. How now, my lord? Isn't it after midnight?

BERTRAM

I have dispatched sixteen matters of business tonight, each should have taken me a month. By an abstract of success: I have met with the Duke, said my adieus to his nearest, bur-   70
ied a wife, mourned for her, wrote to my mother that I am returning, entertained my convoy, and between these main parcels of dispatch affected more delicate errands. The last was the greatest, but is one I have not finished quite yet.

2 DUMAINE

If the business be of any difficulty, with your morning depar- 75
ture, it requires haste of your lordship.

BERTRAM

I mean the business is not ended, I fear we will hear more of it later. But shall we hear this dialogue between the Fool and the Soldier? Come, bring forth this counterfeit model, he has deceived me like a double-meaning prophesier.   80

2 DUMAINE

Bring him here.

Soldiers exit

He's sat in the stocks all night, poor gallant fool.

BERTRAM

It doesn't matter, his heels have deserved it in usurping his spurs for so long. How does he carry himself?

2 DUMAINE

I have told your lordship already the stocks carry him. But   85

to answer you as you would be understood, he weeps like
a woman over spilt milk. He has confessed to Morgan, who
he thinks is a friar, from his earliest of memories to this very
present disaster of his setting in the stocks. And what do you
think he has confessed?   90

BERTRAM

Nothing about me, has he?

2 DUMAINE

His confession is written, and it will be read to his face. If
your lordship is in it, as I believe you are, you must have the
patience to hear it.

Paroles enters, guarded and blindfolded, with the Interpreter

BERTRAM

A plague upon him! Muffled!! He can say nothing about me. 95

1 DUMAINE (*aside to Bertram*)

Hush, hush.

2 DUMAINE (*aside to Bertram*)

The hoodman comes.

(*aloud*) Porto tartarsaucarosa.

INTERPRETER (*to Paroles*)

He calls for the tortures. What will you say?

PAROLES

I will confess what I know without constraint. If you pinch 100
me like a pasty I can say no more.

INTERPRETER

Bosko chicharon.

1 DUMAINE

Boblibindo chimichurri.

INTERPRETER

You are a merciful general. Our general bids you answer the
questions I will ask you.   105

PAROLES

Of course, as I hope to live.

INTERPRETER (*reads*)

"First demand of him how many horse the Duke is strong."

— What do you say to that?

PAROLES

Five or six thousand, but very weak and unserviceable. The troops are all scattered and the commanders very poor 110 rogues, upon my reputation and credit, and as I hope to live.

INTERPRETER

Shall I write this down as your answer?

PAROLES

Do. I'll swear to it, how and which way you will.

BERTRAM (*aside*)

It's all the same to him. What an ass-saving fraud he is!

1 DUMAINE (*aside*)

You're deceived, my lord. This is Monsieur Paroles, the "gal- 115 lant militarist" — that was what he said — that had the whole theory of war in the knot of his scarf, and the practice in the metal mounting of his dagger's sheath.

2 DUMAINE (*aside*)

I will never trust a man again just because he keeps his sword clean, nor will I believe he can have everything just because 120 he is well dressed.

INTERPRETER (*to Paroles*)

Well, we have that written down.

PAROLES

"Five or six thousand horse," I said — I will say true — "or thereabouts" put that down, for I'll speak the truth.

1 DUMAINE (*aside*)

He's very near the truth in this. 125

BERTRAM (*aside*)

But I won't give him credit for it because of the nature in which he delivers the information.

PAROLES

"Poor rogues", write that down.

INTERPRETER

Well, that's in the books.

PAROLES

I humbly thank you, sir. A truth's a truth. The rogues are very 130 poor.

INTERPRETER (*reads*)

"Demand of him of what strength they are on foot." — What do you say to that?

PAROLES

By my word, sir, if I were to die this very hour, I will tell the truth. The muster file, rotten and sound, upon my life 135 amounts to no more than fifteen thousand men, half of the which dare not shake the snow from off their jackets before they shake themselves to pieces.

BERTRAM (*aside*)

What should we do to him?

1 DUMAINE (*aside*)

Nothing, but thank him. (*to Interpreter*) Ask him about me, 140 and what the Duke thinks of me.

INTERPRETER (*to Paroles*)

Well, that's written down. (*reads*) "Ask him, whether one Captain Dumaine, is in the camp, a Frenchman; what his reputation is with the Duke; about his valor, honesty, and expertness in wars; or whether he thinks it possible with well-weighing 145 sums of gold to corrupt him to a revolt." — What do you say to this? What do you know of him?

PAROLES

I ask that you let me answer the particulars of each question. Ask them each separately.

INTERPRETER

Do you know this Captain Dumaine?   150

PAROLES

I know him. He was a tailor's apprentice in Paris, where he was whipped for getting the sheriff's stupid daughter pregnant — an innocent dummy that could not say no to him.

BERTRAM (*aside to 1 Dumaine*)

No, by your leave, sit on your hands, though I know his brains are forfeit to the next shoe that drops.   155

INTERPRETER

Well, is this captain in the Duke of Florence's camp?

PAROLES

Upon my knowledge he is, and lousy.

1 DUMAINE (*aside*)

No, no need to focus on me: We will soon hear about your lordship.

INTERPRETER

What is his reputation with the Duke?   160

PAROLES

The Duke only knows him as a poor officer of mine, and wrote to me the other day to kick him out of the camp. I think I have his letter in my pocket.

INTERPRETER

We will search.

PAROLES

Unfortunately, I do not know. Either it is there, or it is in a file   165
with the Duke's other letters in my tent.

INTERPRETER

Here it is, here's a paper. Shall I read it to you?

PAROLES

I do not know if it be it or not.

BERTRAM (*aside*)

Our interpreter does it well.

1 DUMAINE (*aside*)

Excellently.   170

INTERPRETER (*reads the letter*)

"Diana, the Count's a fool, and full of gold."

PAROLES

That is not the Duke's letter, sir. That is a plea to a proper
maid in Florence, one Diana, to be careful with the advance-
ments of one Count Roussillon, a foolish lazy boy, but for all
that very ruttish. I beg you, sir, put it away.   175

INTERPRETER

No, I'll read it first, with your permission.

PAROLES

My meaning in writing it, I protest, was very honest on the
behalf of the maid, for I knew the young Count to be a dan-
gerous and lascivious boy, who is a shark to virginity, and
devours up all he finds.   180

BERTRAM (*aside*)

Damnable two-faced scoundrel.

INTERPRETER (*reads*)

"When he swears oaths, bid him drop gold, and take it.
After he scores he never pays the score.
Half-won is match well made; match, and well make it.
He never pays after-debts; take it before.
And say a soldier, Diana, told you this: 185
Men are to mess with, boys are not to kiss.
For count on this, the Count's a fool, I know it,
Who pays before, but not when he does owe it.

Yours, as he vowed to you in your ear,

Paroles." 190

BERTRAM (*aside*)

He shall be whipped through the army with this rhyme written on his forehead.

2 DUMAINE (*aside*)

This is your devoted friend, sir, the manifold linguist and the omnipotent soldier.

BERTRAM (*aside*)

I could stand anything before but a rat, and now he's just a 195 rat to me.

INTERPRETER

I perceive, sir, by the general's looks, we shall be forced to hang you.

PAROLES

My life, sir, in any case! Not that I am afraid to die, but that, my offences being many, I would repent out the remainder 200 of my days. Let me live, sir, in a dungeon, in the stocks, or anywhere, just let me live.

INTERPRETER

We'll see what may be done, so long as you confess freely. Therefore once more to this Captain Dumaine. You have answered to his reputation with the Duke, and to his valor. 205 What about his honesty?

PAROLES

He will steal, sir, an egg out of a cloister. For rapes and ravishments he parallels Nessus. He professes not keeping of oaths; in breaking them he is stronger than Hercules. He will lie, sir, with such volubility that you would think truth were a fool. 210 Drunkenness is his best virtue, for he will be swine-drunk, and in his sleep he does little harm, except to his bedclothes; but they know his conditions, and lay him in straw. I have a

little more to say, sir, about his honesty. He has everything
that an honest man should not have; what an honest man 215
should have, he has nothing.

1 DUMAINE (*aside*)

I begin to love him for this.

BERTRAM (*aside*)

For this description of your honesty? Curse him! For me, he's
more and more a rat.

INTERPRETER

What do you say about his expertness in war? 220

PAROLES

Truth, sir, he's led the drum before the English tragedians. I
will not go against him as I do not know more of his soldiership, except in that country he had the honor of being the
officer at a place there called Mile End, to instruct the rank
and file. I would do the man what honor I can, but of this I 225
am not certain.

1 DUMAINE (*aside*)

He has out-villained villainy so far that the rarity redeems
him.

BERTRAM (*aside*)

Curse him! He's still a rat.

INTERPRETER

His qualities being at this poor price, I do not need not to ask 230
you if gold will corrupt him to revolt.

PAROLES

Sir, for a quarter, he would sell his eternal salvation, the
inheritance of it, and cut the entail from all remainders, and
a perpetual succession for it perpetually.

INTERPRETER

What's his brother, the other Captain Dumaine? 235

2 DUMAINE (*aside*)

Why does he ask him about me?

INTERPRETER

What's he?

PAROLES

Birds of a feather. Not altogether so great as the first in goodness, but greater a great deal in evil. He excels his brother for
a coward, though his brother is reputed one of the best there   240
is. In a retreat, he outruns any lackey; but in an attack he
always comes down with cramps.

INTERPRETER

If your life is saved will you be willing to betray the Florentine?

PAROLES

Yes, and the captain of his horse, Count Roussillon.

INTERPRETER

I'll whisper this to the general and find out what he wants.   245

PAROLES

No more drumming. A plague on all drums! Only to seem to
deserve well, and to beguile the supposition of that lascivious
young boy, the Count, have I run into this danger. Yet who
would have suspected an ambush where I was taken?

INTERPRETER

There is no remedy, sir. You must die. The general says that   250
you have so traitorously revealed the secrets of your army,
and made such pestiferous reports of men very nobly held,
you can serve the world no honest use; therefore you must
die. — Come, headsman, off with his head.

PAROLES

Oh Lord, sir! — Let me live, or let me see my death!   255

INTERPRETER

You shall do exactly that. Say goodbye to all of your friends.

(*he takes off Paroles blindfold*)

So, look around you. Know you any here?

BERTRAM

Good day, noble captain.

2 DUMAINE

God bless you, Captain Paroles.

1 DUMAINE

God save you, noble captain.   260

2 DUMAINE

Captain, what greeting will you give to my Lord Lafeu? I am
leaving for France.

1 DUMAINE

Good captain, will you give me a copy of the sonnet you
wrote to Diana on behalf of the Count Roussillon? And if
I were not such a coward I'd force it from you. But fare you 265
well.

All exit all but Paroles and Interpreter

INTERPRETER

You are undone, captain — all but your scarf; that has a knot
in it yet.

PAROLES

Who cannot be crushed with a plot?

INTERPRETER

If you could find out a country where women had received 270
as much shame as you, you might begin an audacious nation.
Fare you well, sir. I am off to France too. We shall speak of
you there.

Interpreter exits

PAROLES

Yet I am thankful. If my heart were great
It would burst at this. Captain I'll be no more,   275
But I will eat and drink and sleep as soft
As captain's shall. Simply the thing I am

Shall make me live. Who knows himself a braggart,
Let him fear this, for it will come to pass
That every braggart shall be found an ass.   280
Rust, sword; cool, blushes; and Paroles live
Safest in shame; being fooled, by foolery thrive.
There's place and means for every man alive.
I'll follow them.

Paroles exits

ACT 4 ♦ SCENE 4

FLORENCE. THE WIDOW'S HOUSE.

Helen, the Widow, and Diana enter

HELEN

So that you can perceive I have not wronged you,
One of the great kings in the Christian world
Will speak for me; I'll need to kneel before
His throne and before I perfect my design.
Time was, I did him a desired favor   5
Dear almost as his life; which gratitude
Through flinty Tartar's bosom would peep forth
And answer "Thanks." I've been duly informed
His grace is at Marseilles, to which place
We have convenient convoy. You should know   10
They think that I am dead. The army breaking,
My husband hurries home, where, heaven aiding,
And by the hand of my good lord the King,
We'll be before our welcome.

WIDOW

Gentle madam,   15
You never had a servant to whose trust
Your business was more welcome.

HELEN

Nor you, mistress,
Ever a friend whose thoughts more truly labor
On repaying you for your love. Doubt not that heaven   20
Has destined me to be your daughter's dower,
As it has fated her to be my motive
And helper to a husband. But oh, strange men,
That can such sweet use make of what they hate,
When saucy trusting of the cozened thoughts   25
Defiles the darkest night; so lust does play
With what it loathes, for that which is away.
But more of this much later. You, Diana,
Under my poor instructions yet must suffer
Something on my behalf.   30

DIANA

Let death and honesty
Go with your impositions, I am yours,
Upon your will to suffer.

HELEN

Yet, I ask you. —
But with the word the time will bring on summer,   35
When briars shall have leaves as well as thorns
And be as sweet as sharp. We must away,
Our wagon is prepared, and time revives us.
All's well that ends well; still the fine's the crown.
Whatever the course, the end is the renown.

They exit

ACT 4 ◆ SCENE 5

ROSSILLION. THE COUNT'S PALACE.

Lavatch, Countess, and Lafeu enter

LAFEU

No, no, no, your son was misled by that snipped-tafetta wearing fellow, whose villainous saffron would have made all the unbaked and doughy youth of a nation in his color. If your daughter-in-law was alive now, and your son here at home, the King would have done more for him than that red-tailed wasp I speak of. 5

COUNTESS

I wish I had never known him. It was the death of the most virtuous gentlewoman that ever nature had praise for creating. If she was born of my flesh and had cost me the dearest groans of a mother I could not have owed her a more rooted love. 10

LAFEU

She was a good lady, she was a good lady. We could pick a thousand salads before we light on such another herb.

LAVATCH

Indeed, sir, she was the sweet marjoram of the salad, or rather the herb of grace. 15

LAFEU

They are not cooking herbs, you buffoon, they are scented flowers.

LAVATCH

I am no great Nebuchadnezzar, sir. I do not have much skill in grass.

LAFEU

What do you call yourself, a knave or a fool? 20

LAVATCH

A fool, sir, at a woman's service, and a knave at a man's.

LAFEU

Your distinction?

LAVATCH

I would do the man a service by servicing his wife.

LAFEU

So you were a knave at his service indeed.

LAVATCH

And I would give his wife my bauble, sir, to do her service.   25

LAFEU

I do declare you are both knave and fool.

LAVATCH

At your service.

LAFEU

No, no, no.

LAVATCH

Why, sir, if I cannot serve you I can serve a prince as great as you.   30

LAFEU

Who's that? A Frenchman?

LAVATCH

Yes, sir, he has an English name, but a face that is hotter in France than here.

LAFEU

What prince is that?

LAVATCH

The Black Prince, sir, alias the Prince of Darkness, alias the   35 Devil.

LAFEU

Hold on, there's my purse. I don't give this to tempt you from your master you talk about; but to serve him still.

LAVATCH

I am a woodland fellow, sir, that always loved a great fire, and the master I speak of always keeps a good fire. But since he is the prince of the world, let the nobility remain in his court; the narrow gate to salvation keeps out the prideful. Some that humble themselves may stoop to enter, but the most will be unable to endure hardship, and they'll elect to go the flowery way that leads to the broad gate and the great fire. 40

45

LAFEU

Go on your way. I am beginning to tire of you, and I tell you so before, because I do not want to fall out with you. Go on your way. Make sure my horses are well looked after, without any tricks.

LAVATCH

If I put any tricks upon them, sir, they shall be worn-out 50 tricks, which are their own right by the law of nature.

Lavatch exits

LAFEU

A sharp-tongue and mischievous rascal.

COUNTESS

So he is. My dead husband liked to joke around with him; by his authority he remains here, which he thinks is a patent for his sauciness, and indeed he has no pace, but runs where 55 he will.

LAFEU

I like him well enough, no offense taken. And I was about to tell you, since I heard of the good lady's death and that my lord your son was upon his return home, I moved the King my master to speak on the behalf of my daughter; which, 60 he himself without prompting proposed. His highness hath promised me to do it; and to stop the displeasure he has conceived against your son, there is no fitter matter. How does your ladyship like it?

COUNTESS

I am very content about it, my lord, and I wish it would happen. 65

LAFEU

His highness comes immediately from Marseilles, as able bodied as when he was thirty. He will be here tomorrow, or I am deceived by a reliable source.

COUNTESS

It gives me great joy that I might be able to see him before I die. I have been told in letters that my son will be here tonight. 70 I beg your lordship to remain with me until they meet.

LAFEU

Madam, I was just thinking how I could politely ask to stay.

COUNTESS

You only need to mention your honorable privilege.

LAFEU

Lady, I have made claims to it before, but, I thank my God, it still holds water. 75

Lavatch re-enters

LAVATCH

Oh madam, my lord your son is over there with a patch of velvet on his face. Whether or not there is a scar under it I don't know, the velvet knows; but it is a good patch of velvet. On his left cheek a beard, but his right cheek is worn bare.

LAFEU

A scar nobly got, or a noble scar, is a good badge of honor. So 80 that is that. (*to the Countess*) Let us go see your son, please. I long to talk with the young noble soldier.

LAVATCH

Well, there's a dozen of them, with delicate fine hats, and most courteous feathers, that bow the head and nod at every man. 85

ACT 5 ◆ SCENE 1

MARSEILLES

Helen, the Widow, and Diana enter, with two attendants

HELEN

But this exceeding travelling day and night
Must wear your spirits low. We cannot help it.
But since you have made the days and nights as one
To wear your gentle limbs in my affairs,
Be reassured I will repay you amply   5
As nothing can unroot you.

A French Gentleman enters

In good time!
This man may help me to his majesty's ear,
If he would spend his power. God save you, sir.

FRENCH GENTLEMAN

And you.

HELEN

Sir, I have seen you in the court of France.   10

FRENCH GENTLEMAN

I have been sometimes there.

HELEN

I do presume, sir, that you are as good
As has been reported they say you are,
And therefore we can skip formalities
Which lay nice manners by, I ask of you
The use of your own virtues for the which   15
I will always be thankful.

FRENCH GENTLEMAN

What do you want?

HELEN

That you will agree

To give this poor petition to the King,

And aid me with that store of power you have

To come into his presence.   20

FRENCH GENTLEMAN

The King's not here.

HELEN

Not here, sir?

FRENCH GENTLEMAN

Indeed he's not.

He hence removed last night, and with more haste

Than is his use.

WIDOW

Lord, all our work for naught.   25

HELEN

All's well that ends well yet,

Though time seem so adverse, and means unfit.

I ask you urgently, where has he gone?

FRENCH GENTLEMAN

I do believe he's gone to Roussillon,

Where I am going now.

HELEN

I ask you, sir,   30

Since you are apt to see the King before me,

Advance the paper to his gracious hand,

Which I presume shall render you no blame,

But rather make you thank your pains for it.

I will come after you with what good speed

Our resources will allow.   35

FRENCH GENTLEMAN (*taking the letter*)

This I'll do for you.

HELEN

And you will find yourself to be well thanked,
Whatever happens. We must mount again.
Go, go, provide.

They exit

ACT 5 ◆ SCENE 2
ROSSILLION. THE COUNT'S PALACE.
Lavatch and Paroles enter, with a letter

PAROLES

Good Master Lavatch, give my Lord Lafeu this letter. I may,
sir, have been better known to you, when I have held famil-
iarity with fresher clothes. But I am now, sir, muddied in
Fortune's mood, and smell somewhat strong of her strong
displeasure.   5

LAVATCH

Truly, Fortune's displeasure is but filthy if it smells as strongly
as you. Please do not block the wind.

PAROLES

You do not need to hold your nose, sir, I was only speaking
in metaphor.

LAVATCH

Indeed, sir, if your metaphor stinks I will hold my nose, or   10
against any man's metaphor. Please step back.

PAROLES

Please, sir, deliver this paper for me.

LAVATCH

Phew, please stand away. A paper from Fortune's toilet to give
to a nobleman! Look, here he comes himself.

Lavatch exits
Lafeu enters

PAROLES

My lord, I am a man whom Fortune has cruelly scratched.   15

LAFEU

And what would you have me do about it? It's too late to clip her nails now. What did you do to play the fool with Fortune that she should scratch you? She herself is a good lady and would not have idiots thrive long under her. There's a silver coin for you. Let the justices make you and Fortune friends; I   20 have other business to attend to.

PAROLES

I beg your honor to give me one single word —

LAFEU

You beg a single penny more. Come, you shall have it. Save your word.

PAROLES

My name, my good lord, is Paroles.

LAFEU

You beg more than one word then. God's passion! Give me   25 your hand. How is your drum?

PAROLES

Oh my good lord, you were the first that found me.

LAFEU

Was I, indeed? And I was the first to lose you.

PAROLES

It lies upon you, my lord, to find me some grace, because of you I lost it.   30

LAFEU

Get out of here, you scoundrel! Do you want to play both God and the Devil? One brings you in grace, and the other brings you out.

(*trumpets sound*)

The King's coming; I know his trumpets. Ask for me later.

I heard talk of you last night. Though you are a fool and a 35
dishonest man, you shall eat. Go on, follow me.

PAROLES

I thank God for you.

They exit

ACT 5 ◆ SCENE 3

THE SAME. ROSSILLION. THE COUNT'S PALACE.

*Flourish of trumpets. The King, Countess, Lafeu, and
the two Dumaines enter with attendants.*

KING

We lost a jewel in her, and ourself worth

Was made much poorer for it. But your son,

As mad in folly, lacked the sense to know

Her worthiness in full.

COUNTESS

That's in the past, my lord, 5

And I beg your majesty to make it

Natural rebellion done in the blade of youth,

When oil and fire, too strong for reason's force,

Overbears it and burns on.

KING

My honored lady, 10

I have forgiven and forgotten all,

Though my revenges were aimed high at him

Waiting for the time to shoot.

LAFEU

This I must say —

But first I beg my pardon — the young lord 15

Did to his majesty, his mother, and his lady

Offense of mighty note, but to himself

The greatest wrong of all. He lost a wife

Whose beauty did astonish the survey
Of richest eyes, whose words all ears took captive,   20
Whose dear perfection made servants humble
Out of proud hearts.

KING

Praising what is lost
Makes remembering dear. Well, call him here.
All is forgiven, and we will squash the past   25
At first view. Let him not ask our pardon;
The nature of his great offense is dead,
We bury deeper than oblivion
The incensing relics of it. Let him approach
A stranger, not offender; and inform him   30
That is how it will be.

ATTENDANT

I will, my lord.

Attendant exits

KING (*to Lafeu*)

What says he to your daughter? Have you spoke?

LAFEU

That he is here to only serve your highness.

KING

Then we shall have a wedding. I sent letters   35
That sets him high in fame.

Bertram enters with a patch of velvet on his left cheek. He kneels.

LAFEU

Well, he looks well.

KING (*to Bertram*)

I am of mixed emotions,
Not a day of season
For you may see a sunshine and a hail   40
In me at once. But to the brightest beams

114

Distracted clouds give way; so stand you forth;
The time is fair again.

BERTRAM

My high-repented blames,
Dear sovereign, please forgive me.   45

KING

All is well.
Not one more word of lost time. Let's move on.
Let's take the instant by the forward top;
For we are old, and the inaudible
And noiseless foot of time can steal away   50
Our quickest decrees. Do you remember
The daughter of this lord?

BERTRAM

Admiringly, my lord. At first,
I stuck my choice on her before my heart
Could make too bold a herald of my tongue;   55
Where, the impression of my eye enfixing,
Contempt his scornful perspective did lend me,
Which warped the line of every other favor,
Stained a fair color or expressed it stolen,
Extended or contracted all proportions   60
To a most hideous object. Then it turned
On she whom all men praised, and whom myself
Since I have lost, have loved, was in my eye
The dust that clouded my judgement.

KING

Well excused.   65
That you did love her strikes some scores away
From the great count. But love that comes too late,
Like a remorseful pardon slowly carried,
To the grace-sender turns a sour offense,

Crying, "That's good that's gone." Our rash faults 70
Make trivial price of the serious things we have,
Not knowing what we have until their grave.
Oft our displeasures, to ourselves unjust,
Destroy our friends and after weep their dust;
Our own love waking cries to see what's done, 75
While shameful hate sleeps out the afternoon.
Be this sweet Helen's knell, and now forget her.
Send your impassioned token for fair Maudlin.
You have our main consent, and here we'll stay
To see our widower's second marriage day. 80

COUNTESS
I hope better than the first. O heavens, bless!
Or ere they meet, in me, O nature, cease.

LAFEU (*to Bertram*)
Come on, my son, in whom my house's name,
Must be digested; give a favor from you
To brighten the spirits of my daughter, 85
So she may quickly come.

(*Bertram gives Lafeu a ring*)
By my old beard
And every hair that's on it, Helen that's dead
Was a sweet creature. Such a ring as this
I saw upon her finger the last time 90
I saw her at court.

BERTRAM
It was not hers.

KING
Now please you let me see it; for my eye,
While I was speaking, often locked on it.

(*Lafeu gives him the ring*)
This ring was mine, and when I gave it to Helen 95

116

    I told her, if she landed in misfortune
    And needed my help, that by this token,
    I would relieve her. Had you the craft to take it from her
    The thing she needed most?

BERTRAM

    My gracious king,   100
    Whatever you may think,
    The ring was never hers.

COUNTESS

    Son, on my life,
    I've seen her wear it, and she valued it
    More than her life.   105

LAFEU

    I am sure I saw her wear it.

BERTRAM

    You are wrong, my lord, she never saw it.
    It was thrown at me from a window in Florence,
    Wrapped in a paper which contained the name
    Of her that threw it. Noble she was, and thought   110
    I stood engaged. But when I had subscribed
    To my own fortune, and informed her fully
    I could not answer in that course of honor
    As she had made the overture, she ceased
    In heavy satisfaction, and would never   115
    Take back the ring again.

KING

    Plutus himself
    The god of riches, the grand alchemist,
    Does not have more of a grasp of nature's
    Mysteries and science than I have in this ring.   120
    Twas mine, twas Helen's. You know it is true.
    Confess it was hers, and by what rough force

You got it from her. She swore to all the saints
That she would never take it off her finger
Unless she gave it to yourself in bed,   125
Where you have never come, or sent it us
Upon her great disaster.

BERTRAM

She never saw it.

KING

On my honor, you are lying
And making me have conjectural fears   130
I would rather shut out. If it should prove
That you are so inhuman — I hope it's not so.
And yet I don't know. You did hate her deadly,
And she is dead, and nothing but to close
Her eyes myself would make me believe   135
More than to see this ring. — Take him away.
My pass suspicions, howe'er the matter fall,
Shall tax my fears of little vanity,
Having vainly fear'd too little. Away with him.
We'll sift this matter further.   140

BERTRAM

If you can prove
This ring was ever hers, you will as easy
Prove that I husbanded her bed in Florence,
Where she never was.

Bertram exits under guard
The French Gentleman enters with a letter

KING

I am wrapped in dismal thoughts.   145

GENTLEMAN

Gracious King,
Whether I have been to blame or no, I know not:

Here's a petition from a Florentine
Who has come short four or five times before
To give it herself. I told her I would deliver it,   150
Influenced by the fair grace and speech
Of the poor petitioner, who by this I know
Is here attending. Her business appears
To be important, and she told me that
In a sweet verbal brief it did concern   155
Your highness and herself.

KING (*reads the letter*)

"Upon his many protestations to marry me when his wife
was dead, I blush to say it, he won me. Now that the Count
Roussillon is a widower, his vows are forfeited to me, and my
honor's paid to him. He stole from Florence, without saying   160
goodbye, and I follow him to his country for justice. Grant it
me, O King! In you it lies best; otherwise a seducer flourishes
and a poor maid is undone. Diana Capilet."

LAFEU

I'd be better off buying a son-in-law in a fair. I'll have nothing
to do with him.   165

KING

The heavens are looking after you, Lafeu,
To bring forth this discovery.
(*to guards*) Seek these suitors.
Go speedily and bring the Count again.

                    Guards exit

I am afraid the life of Helen, lady,   170
Was foully snatched.

                Bertram enters, under guard

COUNTESS

Bring justice on the perpetrators!

KING (*to Bertram*)

 I wonder, sir, if wives are monsters to you,

 And that you fly them as you swear them lordship,

 Why you desire to marry. 175

    The Widow and Diana enter

 Who's that woman?

DIANA

 I am, my lord, a wretched Florentine,

 Descendent of the ancient Capilets.

 My suit you know, as I do understand,

 And therefore know how far I may be pitied. 180

WIDOW (*to the King*)

 I am her mother, sir, whose age and honor

 Both suffer under this complaint we bring,

 And I lose both without your remedy.

KING

 Come here, Count. Do you know these women?

BERTRAM

 My lord, I neither can nor will deny 185

 That I know them. Do they charge me further?

DIANA

 Why do you look so strange upon your wife?

BERTRAM (*to the King*)

 She's no wife of mine, my lord.

DIANA

 If you shall marry

 You give away this hand, and that is mine; 190

 You give away heaven's vows, and those are mine;

 You give away myself, which is known mine,

 For I by vow am so embodied yours

 That she which marries you must marry me,

 Either both or none. 195

LAFEU (*to Bertram*)

Your reputation is not good enough for my daughter, you are
not suited to be her husband.

BERTRAM (*to the King*)

My lord, this is a fond and desperate creature
Whom sometimes I have laughed with. Let your highness
Lay a more noble thought upon my honor   200
Than to think that I would sink to this level.

KING

Sir, as for my thoughts they are not your friends
Until your actions gain my trust. Prove your honor
Is better than what my thoughts imagine.

DIANA

Good my lord,   205
Ask him to swear that he did not take
My virginity.

KING

What do you say to her?

BERTRAM

She's brazen, my lord,
And was a prostitute to the camps.   210

DIANA (*to the King*)

He does me wrong, my lord. If I were so
He might have bought me at a common price.
Do not believe him.

(*Diana takes out Bertram's ring from inside her blouse*)

Oh behold this ring,
Whose high respect and rich validity   215
Is unparalleled; and yet for all that
He gave it to a commoner of the camps,
If I am one.

COUNTESS

    He blushes and is hit.

    That ring, it has been passed and willed by six   220

    Preceding descendants and has been owned

    And worn by the current issue. This is his wife.

    That ring's a thousand proofs.

KING (*to Diana*)

    I thought you said

    You saw one here in court could witness it.   225

DIANA

    I did, my lord, but am loath to produce

    So bad an instrument. His name's Paroles.

LAFEU

    I saw the man, if you could call him that.

KING

    Find him and bring him here now.

Lafeu exits

BERTRAM

    What of him?   230

    He's looked at as a most perfidious fool

    With all the spots of the world taxed and debauched,

    Whose nature sickens but to speak a truth.

    Will I to be judged for this or that by a man,

    Who will say anything?   235

KING

    She has that ring of yours.

BERTRAM

    I grant she has. Certainly I liked her

    And made advances in the wanton way of youth.

    She knew her distance and did angle for me,

    She played hard to get which only made me   240

Want her more; in time
Her infinite cunning with her modern grace
Subdued me to pay her price. She got the ring,
And I had that which my inferior might
Have bought at market price.   245

DIANA

I must be patient.
You who first turned down such a noble wife
Might justly turn away from me. I beg you —
Since you lack virtue I will lose a husband —
Ask for your ring, I will give it back,   250
And give me mine again.

BERTRAM

I don't have it.

KING (*to Diana*)

What ring was yours, might I ask?

DIANA

Sir, much like
The same upon your finger.   255

KING

You've seen this ring? This ring was his of late.

DIANA

Yes. And that is what I gave to him in bed.

KING

The story then is false you threw it to him
From your window?

DIANA

I have spoken the truth.   260

Paroles enters with Lafeu

BERTRAM (*to the King*)

My lord, I do confess the ring was hers.

KING

You shift position shrewdly;

Is this the man you speak of?

DIANA

Yes, my lord.

KING (*to Paroles*)

Tell me, boy — and tell me true, I charge you,   265

Not fearing the displeasure of your master,

Which on your just proceeding I'll keep off —

Of him and this woman what do you know?

PAROLES

May it please your majesty, my master has been an honorable

gentleman. Tricks he has done as gentlemen do.   270

KING

Come, come, get to the point. Did he love this woman?

PAROLES

Yes, sir, he did love her, but how?

KING

Yes, how, tell me?

PAROLES

He did love her, sir, as a gentleman loves a woman.

KING

And how is that?   275

PAROLES

He loved her, sir, and loved her not.

KING

Like how you are an idiot and not an idiot. What an equivo-

cal companion is this!

PAROLES

I am a poor man, and at your majesty's command.

LAFEU (*to the King*)

He's good at making noise, my lord, but a naughty orator.   280

DIANA (*to Paroles*)

Do you know he promised me marriage?

PAROLES

Trust me, I know more than I'll tell.

KING

But you will not tell everything you know?

PAROLES

Yes, if it so pleases your majesty. I carried messages between
them, as I said; but more than that, he loved her, indeed he 285
was mad for her and talked of Satan and of limbo and of
Furies and I don't know what else. Yet I was in with them
at that time so I knew that they were sleeping together and
other proposals, like promising her marriage and things that
would not be proper for me to speak of. Therefore I will not 290
tell all that I know.

KING

You have said everything already, unless you can't say they
are married. But you are too subtle in your evidence, so stand
aside. (*To Diana*) This ring you say was yours.

DIANA

Yes, my good lord. 295

KING

Where did you buy it? Or who gave it you?

DIANA

It was not given, nor did I buy it.

KING

Who lent it to you?

DIANA

It was not lent to me neither.

KING

Where did you find it then? 300

DIANA

I did not find it.

KING

If you did not come by it in these ways,

How could you give it to him?

DIANA

I never gave it to him.

LAFEU (*to the King*)

This woman's an easy glove, my lord, she goes off and on at   305

pleasure.

KING (*to Diana*)

This ring was mine. I gave it to his first wife.

DIANA

It might be yours or hers for all I know.

KING (*to attendants*)

Away with her, I do not like her now.

To prison with her. And away with him. —

Unless you tell me where you got this ring   310

You'll die within this hour.

DIANA

I'll never tell you.

KING (*to attendants*)

Take her away.

DIANA

I'll pay bail, my lord.

KING

I think you now some common prostitute.   315

DIANA (*to Bertram*)

By Jove, if ever I knew man it was you.

KING

So why have you accused him in all this?

DIANA

Because he's guilty, and he is not guilty.

He knows I am no virgin, and he'll swear to it;

I'll swear I am a virgin, and he does not know.   320

Great King, I am no promiscuous woman

I'm either a virgin or else this old man's wife.

KING (*to attendants*)

She is noise in our ears. To prison with her.

DIANA

Good mother, fetch my bail.

Widow exits

Wait, royal sir.   325

The jeweller that owns the ring is sent for,

And they will verify. As for this lord,

Who has abused me as only he knows,

And yet he never harmed me, I quit my claim.

He knows himself my bed he has defiled,   330

And at that time he got his wife with child.

Dead though she be she feels her young one kick.

So there's my riddle; one that's dead is quick.

And now behold the meaning.

Helen and the Widow enter

KING

Is this a spell   335

Beguiles the truer office of my eyes?

Is it real what I see?

HELEN

No, my good lord,

It's just the shadow of a wife you see,

The name and not the thing.   340

BERTRAM

You are both, both. Oh, forgive me!

HELEN

Oh, my good lord, when you thought I was her
I found you wondrous kind. There is your ring.
And look here, there's your letter. This it says:
"When from my finger you can get this ring,   345
And are with child by me." All this is done.
Will you be mine now that you are doubly won?

BERTRAM (*to the King*)

If she, my lord, can make me know this clearly
I'll love her dearly, ever, ever dearly.

HELEN

If it appear not plain and prove untrue,   350
Deadly divorce step between me and you.
Oh my dear mother, do I see you living?

LAFEU

My eyes smell onions, I shall weep soon. (*to Paroles*) Good
Tom Drum, lend me a handkerchief. So, I thank you. Wait on
me home, I'll make sport with you. Let your curtsies alone,   355
they are scurvy ones.

KING (*to Helen*)

We want to take pleasure in hearing this story from begin-
ning to end.
(*to Diana*) If you are still a fresh uncropped flower,
Choose your husband and I'll pay your dower.   360
For I can guess that by your honest aid
You kept a wife a wife, yourself a maid.
Of that and all the progress more and less
Resolvedly more leisure shall express.
All now seems well; and if it end so meet.   365
The bitter past, more welcome is the sweet.

Flourish of trumpets

EPILOGUE

[KING]

The King's a beggar now the play is done.
All is well ended if this suit be won:
That you express content, which we will pay
With strife to please you, every single day.   370
Ours be your patience then, and yours our parts:
Your gentle hands lend us, and take our hearts.

All exit

END OF PLAY